Narcissistic Mothers

A Daughter's Guide to Dealing with Narcissistic Mothers, Recovering From CPTSD, and Healing Emotional Wounds

Linda Hill

© Copyright 2022 - All rights reserved.

The content contained within this book may not be reproduced, duplicated or transmitted without direct written permission from the author or the publisher.

Under no circumstances will any blame or legal responsibility be held against the publisher, or author, for any damages, reparation, or monetary loss due to the information contained within this book, either directly or indirectly.

Legal Notice:

This book is copyright protected. It is only for personal use. You cannot amend, distribute, sell, use, quote or paraphrase any part, or the content within this book, without the consent of the author or publisher.

Disclaimer Notice:

Please note the information contained within this document is for educational and entertainment purposes only. All effort has been executed to present accurate, up to date, reliable, complete information. No warranties of any kind are declared or implied. Readers acknowledge that the author is not engaged in the rendering of legal, financial, medical or professional advice. The content within this book has been derived from various sources. Please consult a licensed professional before attempting any techniques outlined in this book.

By reading this document, the reader agrees that under no circumstances is the author responsible for any losses, direct or indirect, that are incurred as a result of the use of the information contained within this document, including, but not limited to, errors, omissions, or inaccuracies.

Table of Contents

Your Secret Gift #1 1

Introduction 3

Chapter 1: Narcissistic Personality Types & Subtypes 9

    Inside the Mind of the Narcissist 10

    Narcissistic Maternal Parenting Styles 16

    Narcissistic Mother-Daughter Relationship Dynamics 21

    Distinguishing Maternal Narcissistic Signs 26

Chapter 2: Causes of Narcissism and Parenting Manifestations 30

    What Causes NPD? 31

    Parenting Styles 34

    Narcissistic Attachment 39

Chapter 3: Narcissistic Family Dynamics 41

Objectification of the Daughter 41

Narcissistic Control Tools 49

The Effect of Maternal Narcissistic Manifestations............55

Chapter 4: Protection From a Narcissistic Mother 61

Boundaries 62

Taking Back Power..65

Disengagement...71

General Guidelines 76

Chapter 5: Avoiding Toxic Relationships 85

Manifestations and Symptoms of Victimization................86

Managing Attraction..94

Toxic Career Choices, Work Environments, and Coworkers...96

Chapter 6: Re-mothering the Daughter 101

Becoming Your Mother... 103

Re-Mothering the Daughter... 105

Choosing Unconditional Love 112

Banishing the Narcissistic Cycle...................................... 115

Chapter 7: CPTSD Recovery 120

What is CPTSD? 121

Recovery—A Long Term Healing Journey...................... 126

Managing Well-Being 133

Chapter 8: Liberation & Healing Guidelines 137

    The Healing Journey of the Daughter 140

    Grieving the Mother 151

Conclusion 159

    Taking Action to Break the Cycle 160

    Inspiration and Hope 161

Thank You 164

References 165

Linda Hill

Your Secret Gift #1

Get My Next Book

"Narcissistic Mothers - Part 2"

(Free for a limited time)

For a limited time, and as a "Thank you" for purchasing this book, you can be added to our "Book 2 Launch List" for free so you get the second book of this series when it gets published (This book will be priced at $24.99 and I guarantee it will be a great read). Simply visit the URL below and follow the instructions. You'll be the first to get it.

Visit here:

lindahillbooks.com/mothers

Scan QR Code:

Your Secret Gift #2

Get the Audio Version for Free

If you would like to get the audio version of this book so you can read along or listen while you are in the car, walking around, or doing other things, you're in luck. For a limited time, I've provided a link that will allow you to download this audiobook for FREE. (This offer may be removed at any time).

Step 1: Go to the URL below.

Step 2: Sign up for the 30-day free-trial membership (You may cancel at any time after, no strings attached)

Step 3: Listen to the audiobook

Visit here:
lindahillbooks.com/motherspromo

Scan QR Code:

Introduction

Tie up her hands

behind her back

and tell her to love.

The trap of 'trudging' limits a person. The trap of 'clamping' constrains a person. These two words haunt the abused daughters of narcissistic mothers.

When I was younger, I remember watching the movie *A Knight's Tale*, which was based on one of the 24 narrative poems of Chaucer's *Canterbury Tales*, written in the 15th century and published in 1476. Without going into too much detail about the classic book by Chaucer, or the Hollywood version that captured a vast movie audience in 2001, the moral of Chaucer's *Knight's Tale* is that people don't attain what they deserve. I was dumbstruck by the following quote from the actor who portrayed the role of Geoffrey Chaucer in the movie. His words have echoed daily and haunted me for a lifetime since: "Uh… trudging. You know, trudge? To trudge: the slow, weary, depressing yet determined walk of a man who has nothing left in life except the impulse to simply soldier on."

Sometimes one word has the power of summing up a range of feelings that are so profound that no more description is required. While I am trudging on in life, my sister is the one who has had her head clamped for more than half a century. She is being puppeted around without any sign of release. Since her earliest memory, her whole life has been held in an unwanted brace that she cannot escape from. I doubt if she will be released from this trap when our mother meets her grave. It's inside this oppressing scene where we have to breathe and smile at the world (which only sees the delightful stage of our performance and not the truth).

Perhaps this is one of the unconscious reasons why I found the study of psychology a fascinating topic at university. I was able to relate to a multitude of concepts that appeared on the pages of my books. The books made me aware of the dysfunctional patterns that I always interpreted as a normal reality in the vagueness of my daily toil. Even though it took me longer than the average student to complete my degree, I remained focused as I was trudging along in a haze while trying to liberate myself from a world to which I slowly became aware I never belonged.

A half-century has passed in the doubtful world of living a lie and being lied to about living. It took many toxic relationships and work environments to reach the point where my eyes opened up to an evasive reality after I suffered intense abuse at the hands of a person that I loved and trusted completely. After a very painful breakup with my life partner, I found solace in the words of Sylvia Plath: "The floor seemed wonderfully solid. It was comforting to know I had fallen and could fall no farther" (Plath, 1963, p. 40).

I am filled with emotion when I reflect on my life, my choices, my habits, and my responses to other significant others. Feelings of shame, regret, and profound grief overwhelm me. I have experienced all the stages of continuous trauma during a life that feels like a constant battle for survival. It has been a daily struggle to keep breathing and continue. I feel robbed of a life, of innocence, and of tranquility. And I blame my narcissistic mother for this.

What is narcissism? The term is derived from the mythological figure Narcissus whose excessive self-love for his reflection caused his demise. *Britannica* (Rhodewalt, 2019) defines narcissism as "an inflated self-image and addiction to fantasy" that is characterized by "an unusual coolness and composure shaken only when the narcissistic confidence is threatened, and to the tendency to take others for granted or to exploit them." This sounds like my mother. And the worst tragedy is that she doesn't even realize or acknowledge this fact. Nobody ever dared to threaten her harmony or her authority!

According to Sigmund Freud, narcissistic tendencies are normal during childhood but become a threat when the behavior continues beyond puberty, when it can be identified as a disorder. A narcissist will constantly coerce others to enhance their already highly inflated self-esteem. According to her self-concept, my mother was (and still is) always the best person in the room, she remains the most knowledgeable person on any topic, she is still the same 19-year-old girl with the smallest hips and most beautiful legs even though she hovers on reclining into old age. In her eyes, nobody can match her achievements. She also remains the reason for and owner of all the achievements that my sister and I managed to obtain to please her as she garnered them in her own esteem.

It took me many years to identify and understand the toxicity of the maternal environment I was exposed to. After years of therapy and rebuilding my self-image, I am able to identify and introduce boundaries where necessary so that I can finally start living. My goal is to share my experience through this book and if I am able to touch another suffering person's soul by relating this painful topic, then I will find release. If you find yourself in that desperate position, you have found the right book to guide you on your healing path. Together we can meander on the journey of recovery by reaching an understanding of the entrapment of narcissistic maternal abuse, setting up boundaries, and releasing overwhelming emotions. If you come to realize that your trauma manifested in a different way then I hope that you are able to apply some of the concepts toward a more restorative existence. We all have a right to be fully alive.

I have learned that the first step to healing is to find hope. This book will provide hope. We will benefit together en route to a newly found hope by broadening our understanding of maternal narcissism. Knowledge sets us free. Understanding why and how the mind of a narcissistic mother operates will help us to forgive and ultimately guide us to find more healthy patterns of response. I would like to offer the prospect of change to you from these pages because when we cannot change someone else, we always have the power to change ourselves and our viewpoints. This is the liberation that we should aim for.

"Nature and nearby woods offered me a safe place to be. I used to play in the woods often alone. I thrived smelling the woods only because nothing in there intimidated or blamed me" (Jabeen et al., 2021).

Let's breathe again. Let's breathe together.

Chapter 1

Narcissistic Personality Types & Subtypes

Dearest Father,

You asked me recently why I maintain that I am afraid of you. As usual, I was unable to think of any answer to your question, partly for the very reason that I am afraid of you, and partly because an explanation of the grounds for this fear would mean going into far more detail than I could even approximately keep in mind while talking. And if I now try to give you an answer in writing it will still be very incomplete, because, even in writing, this fear and its consequences hamper me in relation to you and because the magnitude of the subject goes far beyond the scope of my memory and power of reasoning. —Franz Kafka

These harrowing words are from Kafka's letter to his narcissistic father. To understand the mind of a narcissistic parent, we have to understand how they think and perceive the world. In this chapter, we will look at psychological disorders and explore the differences between the subtypes of narcissistic personality disorder (NPD). Personality disorders are identified by chronic, inflexible, and maladaptive patterns that have a negative impact on relationships. These patterns are perceivable in the person's thoughts, behaviors, and emotions. NPD is often associated with comorbidities of other psychological orders.

Inside the Mind of the Narcissist

The Diagnostic and Statistical Manual for Mental Disorders (DSM-IV and the revised DSM-5) defines NPD as "a pervasive pattern of grandiosity (in fantasy or behavior), need for admiration, and lack of empathy, beginning by early adulthood and present in a variety of contexts" (DSM-IV and DSM-5 Criteria for the Personality Disorders, 2012). The individual must furthermore present at least five of the following criteria to be diagnosed with NPD:

- An exaggerated sense of self-importance and superiority despite relatable achievements
- A preoccupation with fantasies of unlimited success and power, brilliance and beauty, or ideal love

- An inflated belief that the individual is exceptional, only understood by high-status individuals, and should only associate with other superior people

- Excessive demand for constant admiration

- A high degree of entitlement and demanding automatic compliance and agreement with these expectations

- Taking advantage of others in an exploitive way in order to attain personal goals

- A complete lack of empathy and unwillingness to recognize and understand the feelings of others

- Profound feelings of envy. The envy can be directed toward others but it can also be a belief that others envy them

- Arrogant and patronizing attitudes and behaviors

The narcissistic individual thus shows definite impairments in personality and interpersonal functioning. These should not be caused by substance abuse. It should be stable and consistent across different scenarios and interactions, and it should not be dependent on socio-cultural or developmental factors.

NPD shows some similar traits to other personality disorders like borderline, avoidant, and paranoid personality disorder. Since many people show a set of narcissistic personality traits, we should make a distinction between the diagnosis of a personality disorder and a purely narcissistic person. The narcissist does not even think about the traits that appear narcissistic to them or others. Their primary objective is to gain power, money, and prestige. I can think of a few well-known politicians in this arena… On the other hand, an individual diagnosed with the mental disorder NPD shows many of the same traits but underneath the surface, they suffer intense feelings of shame, low self-esteem, and humiliation. They, therefore, fluctuate constantly between emotions of superiority and feeling plain miserable. These people generally cannot function well and they alienate family members, friends, and social connections. They also suffer from depression because of their resulting isolation.

The dynamics in play inside the narcissist's mind manifest in the following ways. Their interpersonal actions show a powerful negative impact because of their lack of insight and understanding of the perspective of others. Narcissists interpret behavior differently and they often feel misunderstood. They act deviously. Pathological lying to justify their perceptions is common because they believe they deserve things, and they believe a different truth from reality. They cannot separate the feeling from the truth. They find it difficult to refrain from a specific behavior instead of changing the undesired behavior.

NPD is categorized into two distinct types, namely grandiose (or overt) narcissism and vulnerable (or covert) narcissism.

Overt Narcissistic Personality Disorder

The overt NPD exhibits extreme signs of grandiosity. These individuals are arrogant and socially bold. They display superficial charm, high levels of confidence, and manifest signs of callousness. Grandiose narcissists show aggression, external anger, envy, and they harbor fantasies of power and wealth. They are generally extroverted individuals who appear unemotional and show a complete lack of insight.

Covert Narcissistic Personality Disorder

Vulnerable narcissists are more difficult to identify because their narcissistic behaviors are hidden and not obvious. They often display hypersensitivity when being criticized. They are resentful and distrusting of others, and their insecurity is rooted in underlying shame issues. They are often introverted and generally suffer from anxiety and depression. Paranoia, neuroticism, defensiveness, and pessimism are rife. They are avoidant and socially awkward, and their fragile self-esteem is obvious. They come across as cold and distant, and unforgiving. In contrast to overt narcissists, they internalize anger issues. They can be oblivious but most importantly, they require a constant feed of attention and will go out of their way to acquire this.

Which Narcissistic Subtype Is Worse?

Narcissistic abuse causes far-reaching harm, creating emotional numbness and emotional rejection. It is generally believed that narcissism cannot be changed, but covert NPD has a slightly higher recovery rate—if help is sought. People with narcissistic tendencies generally do not think they need help because they do not believe that something is wrong. When we compare the subtypes, we find the following tendencies toward change.

The subtypes may present in different ways in different environments but covert narcissists are more attuned to sadness and also manifest more possibility to change because of their lack of confidence, their concept of underlying shame, and their poor self-deception. They fight off attacks from others that they take personally whereas overt narcissists are resistant to criticism and are able to deflect attacks more easily. The shame issue gives the vulnerable narcissist the feeling that they are bad—they understand that something is wrong even though they cannot identify what it is. So, they show a little more insight even though both subtypes remain highly resistant to change. Shame is based on the concept that "I am bad" as opposed to "being actually wrong." This differs from feelings of guilt that are based on facts. Therapy that is based on shame work can therefore improve narcissistic tendencies because the covert narcissist shows slightly more insight that makes them fall back on their poor self-image.

Recovery also depends on the difference in fantasies and envy between the two subtypes. With grandiose narcissists, envy is more evident but the narcissist does not know why and they act oblivious. They persist in showing externalized anger and aggression, without a sense of forgiveness because their lack of insight prohibits their violation concept. (They actually believe they did nothing wrong.)

The most obvious vulnerable narcissistic traits (resentfulness, paranoia, shame, hypersensitivity, pessimism, insecurities, avoidance, social awkwardness, coldness, and distancing) make the covert narcissist unforgiving because they cannot forgive themselves, so it is also not easy to forgive others. They internalize anger and avoid confrontation. Because they feel inferior, they are aware of their jealousy (and the reasons why they feel jealous) but still find it difficult to change their behavior. This creates a strong association with sadness.

The worst damage happens through narcissistic communication. All communication is based on feelings.

For the narcissist to change, they must focus on communication-based decisions instead of feeling-based decisions. They must learn to consider the consequences and not simply react instinctively. Change is thus probable when a therapist assists them with reflective communication prior to reactive communication styles. Therapeutic intervention that ultimately focuses on communication issues (delivery of their message, abstaining from lying, checking in with people's emotions) could benefit the narcissist.

The true narcissist does not think about themselves as being narcissistic and does not identify or understand the narcissistic traits. They do not realize that these factors affect others. This is why changing their behavior is the key to changing the narcissist. Narcissistic thoughts are automatic, and narcissistic feelings are also automatic, but narcissistic behavior can be prevented. It is difficult to change a feeling and a thought but changing behavior is easier. The challenge is that most individuals with narcissistic tendencies do not believe that they need assistance to improve their behavior.

Narcissistic Maternal Parenting Styles

Dealing with a narcissistic individual is probably the most difficult when that person is a parent. The mother is supposed to be the one person that a child can trust and depend upon for healthy guidance. When the mother shows narcissistic tendencies, she fails you in the worst possible way.

There are eight prominent mothering patterns. Most of these mothering patterns portray significant narcissistic elements. Because all children automatically rely on their mothers for basic needs and nurturing, dysfunctional interactions from these patterns will form lifelong problems and trigger archetypal (conditioned) responses in the victim later in life. The common denominator in inattentive motherhood is a lack of empathy, which is something very unique to NPD types.

It's important to note that an imperfect mother can still present a healthy relationship dynamic. The danger of a dysfunctional connection arises from repetitive patterns that are never acknowledged or corrected. A light of hope is that evolution gave the stronger and more powerful need for survival to the child and not the mother.

- Dismissive parenting style

    The dismissive motherhood style ranges on a spectrum from ignoring the child's needs to complete abandonment. The mother may ask the daughter what she would like to eat and without listening to the response, simply provide something else. The dismissal could turn into abandonment by never asking the daughter how she is feeling or simply never acknowledging her presence. In both ways, the daughter becomes irrelevant to the mother as she continues in her self-absorbed life. The mother's withdrawal can ultimately become complete denial on her part.

- Enmeshed parenting style

    The relationship between mother and daughter becomes a 'chokehold' as the mother does not acknowledge boundaries between them. She fiercely 'lives' through the life of her daughter and the connection between them becomes a staged life for all to see. This entrapment exploits the concept of unconditional love and human nature and uses 'love' to attain ulterior goals. All the healthy developmental stages of the daughter get swallowed up and her self-awareness gets trapped in a no-release situation that is very difficult to correct later in life.

- Combative parenting style

    Hypercritical, competitive, and jealous mothers are examples of a mean powerplay in the mother-daughter dynamic. These mothers not only display their power over a child but also determine how the child is supposed to interpret the world. Blaming and shaming are the obvious weapons used by the mother, and the daughter never releases her own sense of responsibility for making mistakes or making the mother feel bad. The abuse can be verbal, emotional, and physical and regardless of the method, it remains a devastating path for the child's future. A deep sense of unworthiness develops.

- Controlling parenting style

    The mother micromanages the daughter and does not acknowledge the validity of the child's choices and actions. She controls the daughter under the impression of doing things for the child's "own good" but it actually says that the daughter has impaired judgment and she is inadequate to make decisions on her own. This leads to helplessness and insecurity in adulthood.

- Unavailable parenting style

    The mother actively withdraws from the child and becomes emotionally disconnected. She avoids physical intimacy and never comforts the daughter. Sometimes she will even withhold connection from one child but give it to another. It's excruciatingly painful for the child and leaves the daughter bewildered and unsure. The child becomes a clingy adult with insecure attachments that require copious amounts of reassurance.

- Unreliable parenting style

   Never knowing if the "good mother" or the "bad mother" will appear creates one of the most dangerous and difficult relationship dynamics to cope with. As an adult, the victimized daughter always struggles with trust in relationships and regards them all as precarious journeys to take on the road of emotional connection. This spiteful attitude of the mother leaves the child with a constant "voice in her head" and tremendous insecurity.

- Self-involved parenting style

   The daughter is simply an extension of the mother. She has no right to a life of her own. The mother controls the child in devious ways to suit her own needs and to achieve her own goals, never acknowledging the daughter. Her power play is devoid of empathy and she manipulates the daughter purely to feel good about herself and her own grandiosity. These mothers appear charming and talented while the daughters suffer from being unloved, and the relationship is devoid of sincerity.

- Role-reversed parenting style

    In this scenario, the daughter becomes the 'mother' and caretaker. Circumstances that may enhance this are when the mother had her children at a young age, coupled with too many children at the same time, or perhaps additional financial demands that do not allow her to be an attentive mother. It could also be a result of a mother's chronic illness or depression. Often the older child automatically takes over the role of mother and is never able to liberate herself from this position. The daughter may feel robbed of her childhood as an adult. In many cases though, the daughter can heal after therapeutic intervention when reconciliation and understanding are reached.

The most disturbing effect of dysfunctional parenting styles appears when the narcissistic mother becomes a constant voice inside the daughter's head. The narcissistic parent wreaks havoc that causes a lifetime of suffering and cognitive distortion that is not easy to correct.

Narcissistic Mother-Daughter Relationship Dynamics

Let's look at some typical narcissistic mother-daughter

dynamics. The narcissistic mother's conditional love depends on the child's response or performance to the mother's whims. She wants a worthy audience, and the child is an easy target. Three of the most prominent narcissistic mothering styles manifest as follows in the daughter.

Incompetent Childhood

With an incompetent childhood, the daughter experiences nullification. She is never appreciated or supported. Eventually, the daughter gives up on her important goals. Her values and activities are always ridiculed and never tolerated. A typical example of this is when a daughter tries to be useful to the mother and always chooses arguments that she knows the mother will win.

She also experiences ambiguities in the demonstration of power. The mother always determines what is right and permitted. There is a continued perception of dissatisfaction from the mother enabling a trapped daughter who constantly feels humiliated. This demonstrates a cruel level of power where no boundaries between mother and daughter are established, and the daughter never knows what to expect next. The daughter may end up always wearing clothes the mother chooses because her choices are ugly or unacceptable in the mother's eyes.

The daughter may experience shame because her identity is formed on a basis of inferiority, weakness, imperfection, and ineffectiveness. She feels worthless and frames her life as one of service and suffering. She ends up trying to be non-existent and obedient in order to please and pacify the mother.

Denied Childhood

In a denied childhood scenario, the daughter is exposed to a deeply threatening environment. She may have a constant fear of making the mother angry, and therefore learn to be highly vigilant and careful of what she says or does. She lives in constant terror, constantly assuring the mother how good she is in order to keep the peace. A typical response from a denied childhood daughter is "I kept my mother in a good mood."

The daughter may also experience rejection. She may have no protection, she may be forgotten or ignored, and no basic safety is provided by the mother. Sometimes the mother will also allow others to mistreat the daughter without interfering or acknowledging any damage caused. One such example is where the daughter commented in therapy that her toys were taken away because she was told at the age of nine that she was too old to play.

Violence often results in denied childhood dynamics even without any provocation. The mother takes it as her responsibility to always punish the daughter, regardless of the circumstances. The effect of this is that the child is afraid all the time.

Isolated Childhood

In an isolated childhood, dependence becomes an issue. The mother makes sure that the daughter depends on her, she limits her interaction with others, and all energy is focused on the mother. The daughter must satisfy the endless needs of the mother and, like in a black hole, the inescapable presence of the mother never leaves. Concepts of triangulation (often with other siblings or another parent) and secrecy prevail. The mother may for example never say positive things about others. Blaming without reason or logic happens frequently and the daughter gets blamed for everything. The mother-daughter relationship never stabilizes into trust, and the daughter never knows when she is manipulated or when things are real.

Creating a shining facade for the outside world takes place in this dynamic. The mother tries to satisfy her feelings of envy by making sure the home is always perfect. The mother takes all the credit for this. There is only an appearance of perfection to others while the mother's inner chaos remains a deep secret. She despises others and it manifests in an ambiguous real misery versus the appearance of a perfect fantasy to others. The daughter is denied happiness unless the happiness is related to the mother's happiness. Most often these daughters comment that they can never tell their mother about their happiness and outsiders never imagined the real nightmare at play inside the secrecy.

Regardless of the specific mother-daughter dynamics, some characteristics occur consistently. Narcissistic mothers are highly condescending parents. Choices betray the narcissist so they make the child believe they have a choice while they actually don't. They are controlling and manipulating mothers who require no validation as they embark on a journey of guilt-tripping. They divert the daughter's problems to their own, compete with the daughter, violate boundaries, make the daughter feel like a burden with a "debt to be repaid," and encourage mistreatment or punishment of the daughter by others. They are generally merciless and cruel. They are emotionally unavailable or give the wrong emotional availability.

The effects of the dynamics are devastating. All the above lead to victim shame. An incompetent childhood dynamic leads to inferiority and worthlessness. An isolated childhood creates a hypervigilant adult who turns against other people and focuses on the mother. A denied childhood results in insecurity and intense feelings of fear. In general, the results are insecure attachments and a greater risk of developing psychopathology. The dysfunctional parenting of maintaining an unhealthy self-image narrative, refusal to get help, avoidance of inconvenience, and complete lack of humility attacks the daughter's thought processes and causes emotional distress. The mother's incapability of admitting mistakes, ignorance of the truth, demands for unrealistic perfection, and remorseless lying enable trust issues in the daughter's life.

Distinguishing Maternal Narcissistic Signs

These mothers are always diverting the conversation to themselves because their problems are always 'worse.' Instead of getting support, the daughter gets criticism when she voices her problems. The narcissistic mother wants to make the daughter believe that she is a failure, that she is worthless and it's the daughter's fault. The daughter must meet the needs of the mother and this is her sole reason for being. Narcissistic mothers tend to show the following distinguishable signs.

- She competes with the daughter, the boyfriend, or the father. The daughter will never be good enough, she is inferior to the mother.

- She makes the daughter feel like a burden as if she should never have been born. This is a common and very cruel characteristic of narcissistic mothers.

- She fails to protect her daughter from someone who causes harm to her. She does not care and even enjoys observing the mistreatment of the daughter.

- Emotional unavailability or the wrong emotional availability are common signs. She easily makes too much of the daughter's emotions and eventually, the daughter abstains from sharing emotions for fear of them getting twisted in the mother's perspective.

- She is a controlling and manipulative mother. Guilt-tripping and blowing everything out of proportion happen frequently. Sometimes these signs are not verbal but simply a facial expression of disappointment. Her behaviors are not authentic.

- The daughter can never repay her 'debt' and she must be impressed by the sacrifice the mother made. She is accused of being ungrateful if she doesn't show gratitude to the mother and she is a disappointment in the eyes of the mother.

- No unconditional love or true approval develops. The daughter always has to gain love from performance.

- Boundary violations are common. The mother allows no privacy and enforces judgments. She puts the daughter down in front of others.

It is not easy to escape from a narcissistic mother. Even after the mother's death, the daughter may still suffer from the effects of continuous mistreatment and dysfunctional interaction. The daughter may always struggle with shame, never trust her inner voice or her own abilities, and have difficulty setting healthy boundaries. She may experience anger issues. She may feel incompetent, uncertain, and hypersensitive throughout her life. It's a highly destructive dynamic and the daughter learns not to trust anyone on an intimate level. The mother's voice reigns supreme until the daughter decides to break free.

Takeaway Guidelines

- Exploitation, superiority, lack of empathy, and an excessive need for admiration are some of the main characteristics of narcissism.

- Two distinct types of narcissism exist, namely

grandiose narcissism and vulnerable narcissism.

- Narcissistic abuse causes extensive harm and creates emotional scarring, especially because of dysfunctional communication patterns.

- Most mothering styles portray significant narcissistic elements.

- The narcissistic mothering styles mostly create a denied, incompetent, or isolated childhood with distinguishable signs.

- Constant victim-shaming results in insecure attachments and resulting psychopathologies.

Calls to Action

- Familiarize yourself with the concept of narcissism.

- Seek professional help to rebuild your confidence.

- Shame-work therapy is highly beneficial.

Chapter 2

Causes of Narcissism and Parenting Manifestations

In an article published in 2020 about narcissistic traits in young people, the researchers van Schie et al. found that,

> "Cold and indifferent parenting may hamper the development of an adaptive self-view. It has been postulated that a lack of mirroring through cold parenting could contribute to the child's failure to master a normal developmental process whereby a grandiose self is replaced with a more realistic view of the self. However, too much mirroring through being overly sensitive to a child's need (e.g., overparenting or pampering) is thought to be problematic as well, making people more reliant on others for feedback and guidance."

Their research results concluded that overvaluing and lenient parenting styles were mostly responsible for narcissistic characteristics in young people. It also became evident from their research that maladaptive attachment issues on a spectrum of extremes (instead of a balanced scenario) are the basic causes of narcissistic development. Sigmund Freud also proposed that a combination of parental overvaluation together with a lack of empathy (awareness of the child's needs) are to be blamed for increasing narcissistic development. Because narcissistic behavior exhibits such a wide range of severity, many children who become aware of their exposure to narcissistic parenting live with the fear of becoming narcissistic themselves. In this chapter, I will try to present an understanding of the root causes and manifestations of narcissism.

What Causes NPD?

Narcissistic characteristics are normal stages of early

human development, but when the traits persist and cause dysfunction in various areas of the person's life and interactions, the devastating outcomes are alarming. Researchers are still unsure about the causes of NPD and it is, therefore, better to say that some scenarios and factors are 'associated' with NPD and not the "definite cause" of NPD. Paternal versus maternal narcissistic parenting styles also have different manifestations in the child's development and narcissistic displays in adult life.

Most theories are based on significant links to unhealthy child-parent relationships in early developmental phases. There is no strong genetic link to the development of narcissism, so most scientists agree that a combination of social, psychological, environmental, and biological factors contribute to narcissism. Mostly overly protective or neglectful parenting styles determine the outcome. The following theories remain the most popular.

Inheritability

According to Dr. Todd Grande, about 40–65% of narcissistic characteristics are inherited (Grande, 2018). He bases this on the fact that learned behavior from narcissistic parents, together with the potential harm done by narcissistic parents who are unable to regulate and recognize emotions, hamper the child's emotional awareness development. As a result, the child generally depends on other people to help them identify and regulate their own underdeveloped emotional awareness.

Genetics

In other studies, the narcissistic traits of entitlement and grandiosity showed a higher correlation to genetic inheritance in research than the classification of narcissism in general. This is based on test results from Chinese researchers monitoring twins, where tests showed independent results from environmental influences (Mandal, 2010). Structural changes and brain differences have not been consistently identified in other research, but correlated sections identified in the brain are responsible for social behavior and emotional regulation.

Environmental Factors

Inconsistent childhood environments and childhood experiences are more associated with an increased risk of narcissism. The extremes of excessive praise and/or criticism coupled with a definite imbalance may cause narcissistic tendencies. When these co-exist with a lack of parental empathy, unrealistic praise for appearance or abilities (overvaluation), and an emphasis on success and status, narcissistic tendencies are enhanced. Emotional abuse or neglect, together with inconsistent and authoritarian parenting that lacks supervision, inhibit the child's abilities to regulate emotions, leaving her with confused and avoidant attachment patterns later in life.

Social and Developmental Factors

The Austrian psychoanalysts Heinz Kohut and Otto Kernberg (Rhodewalt, 2019) maintain the theory that disturbances in early childhood social interactions with the parental figure (specifically the mother) determine the development of NPD in the child. Stunted development of the healthy self creates a favorable environment for narcissistic tendencies when unsatisfactory social relationships cultivate unhealthy conflicting psychological dependence later in life.

Apart from developmental interactions, the 21st century also contributes to community and social issues on the enhancement of narcissistic tendencies. Studies about social media usage frequency and upload ease and volume, are still inconsistent and in their beginning stages, but the studies do show a significant prevalence of narcissistic tendencies. These may be aggravated by narcissistic parenting styles and similarities. The pathological use of social networking sites appears to be an enabling environment for communicating narcissistic needs and achieving narcissistic goals. Although social studies show inconsistencies with regards to narcissistic behavior, it is evident that social networking sites do offer a significant correlation with these tendencies and an outlet to satisfy narcissistic needs, particularly grandiose narcissistic presentations.

Parenting Styles

It is not clear if any specific parenting styles lead to

grandiose narcissism but a positive correlation to vulnerable narcissism exists. The Van Schie study proved that overprotective parental styles showed a higher correlation to the development of both vulnerable and grandiose narcissism, primarily because it limits the child's ability to learn from their own mistakes, make autonomous decisions, and remain dependent on the guidance and feedback of other people. It also elevates more negative self-beliefs in the child, which in turn discourages future adult independence.

Overvaluation is associated with grandiose narcissism because of inflated and unrealistically positive self-views by the children whose parents' subjective views of their achievements and success contribute to a distorted image of reality. Being praised, despite true achievement or deliberate effort, enables cheating or avoidant tactics in order to sustain a positive self-image. It is thus evident that a pure lack of care is not the sole reason for the development of narcissistic characteristics.

Invalidating a child's needs was also found to enable narcissistic development during research studies. However, having another parent who counters the narcissistic parent by providing care, enables different levels and manifestations of narcissistic tendencies in the child. Maternal leniency is more correlated to the development of vulnerable narcissism while paternal leniency and overvaluation are more associated with grandiose narcissistic development. Maternal parenting is also more closely linked to narcissistic developments, while paternal factors are linked to specific scenarios.

It is crucial to be aware that childhood maltreatment can be a risk factor in the development of many personality disorders, not only NPD.

Authoritative Parenting

The authoritative mother uses reasoning or explanation to influence the child. She is assertive (not intrusive) and assumes the child's rights. This is the healthiest parenting style and combines a balance of setting healthy limits with warmth and sensitivity toward the child. Positive reinforcement instead of punishment guides the child's behavior. The benefit is that the child becomes independent and a socially accepted adult who displays academic success later in life. These children are also less likely to develop comorbidities like anxiety and depression or show antisocial and delinquent behavior.

Authoritarian Parenting

The authoritarian mother maintains control. She expects obedience and uses this manipulation to shape the child. No explanations are necessary or required for her actions as she follows the clear command-punishment parenting style. This parenting style shows a lot of psychological control and less nurturing. It is fear-based and controlling while demanding blind submission to authority. The goal is to break the will of the child and reshape her into a standardized object. Control is managed through shaming, withholding love, and strict punishment.

This style is positively correlated to the development of narcissism in a maternal parenting scenario. It generally leads to poor performance in adulthood. Depending on various cultural contexts, this style also creates distance between the parent and child who experiences the connection as 'cold'.

Permissive Parenting

The permissive mother is more lenient, and she does not expect (nor desire) maturity from the child. She is overly affective and struggles to punish the daughter. This inhibits the development of the child into a healthy adult. This style is often referred to as an indulgent parenting style and the focus is on being nurturing and warm. This has its positive outcomes but the general lack of imposing limits or healthy boundaries is problematic. These parents refuse to control their children. The problems arise from the fact that the child is not being guided to regulate herself and is not given adult tasks or expected to mature. The main communication strategy from these parents is manipulative instead of direct because they do not see themselves as authority figures in the child's development. This style shows a negative correlation to vulnerable narcissistic development. The child becomes a resourceful adult with high self-esteem but generally shows a lack of self-discipline and responsibility. Research has shown increased aggression, a higher likelihood of misconduct, and lower levels of academic achievement with permissive parenting.

Indifferent Parenting

The child of the indifferent mother is encouraged to be totally independent of the parent. She is given no support and thus has to take responsibility for everything herself. She is mainly left to her own devices. It is also known as uninvolved parenting. The parent is detached and emotionally disengaged and distant from the child. The child is neglected, and the parent is dismissive, unresponsive, and indifferent while making no demands on the child. No rules are set and no boundaries are encouraged. The parent shows no interest in the child's life and this is often caused by her own overwhelming problems that take priority. Sometimes parental substance abuse issues or chronic depression may be the cause of uninvolved parenting.

The outcome of the child's development shows poor

performance at nearly every level of the child's adult life. These children show a severe lack of social skills, poor cognitive development, dysfunctional emotional skills, and continuous attachment issues. They are often anxious and stressed, show delinquency during adolescence, often abuse substances, and fear becoming dependent on other people.

Narcissistic Attachment

Narcissistic attachment is extremely destructive. Narcissists can attach to a spouse, a business partner, a friend, a parent, or the child. The golden child becomes the narcissistic parent's endless supply of admiration and appreciation that feeds their self-worth and confidence. Eventually, the victimized child becomes exhausted from all the energy that the narcissist drains from them. The child and the parent become one and this inhibits the maturation of healthy independent development. Focus changes, identity is lost. It enables a false sense of superiority and engenders a deep sense of rejection. The child is constantly walking on eggshells and fears emotional or envious outbursts from the narcissistic parent.

How do we prevent becoming the narcissistic parent to our own children after being exposed to years of traumatizing, conditioning, and victimization? I believe it starts with an understanding of narcissism, followed by taking back your power. The stronger you become, the weaker her control becomes.

Takeaway Guidelines

- Factors associated with the development of NPD are mostly based on unhealthy child-parent relationships in early developmental phases.

- Neglect or excessive appraisal are the most prominent warning signs for narcissistic development.

- Four distinguishable parenting signs exhibit relatable symptoms in the development of the child, namely authoritative, authoritarian, permissive, and indifferent parenting.

- Destructive narcissistic attachment creates boundary confusion and insecure development.

Calls to Action

- Understanding how the narcissistic parent functions gives you the tools to relearn new coping styles and release from toxic maternal control.

- An understanding of the different parental styles enables you to stop the damaging generational spiral of narcissistic behavior.

Chapter 3

Narcissistic Family Dynamics

Maya Angelou wrote in her book, *I Know Why the Caged Bird Sings*, that "There is no greater agony than bearing an untold story inside you" (Curtis, 2018).

A dysfunctional family dynamic with a narcissistic parent wreaks havoc. It damages the children for many years and its legacy is miserable. But it can be changed and reinvented. The change starts with the children, the ones who were the vulnerable victims. The way to do this is to disempower the parent from the siblings, ideally in a situation where the siblings unite and agree to manage the narcissistic tendencies together. In this chapter I will explain these complicated dynamics.

Objectification of the Daughter

A deep violation of an individual's right to life is objectification. Not only does this happen in romantic relationships, for example, when a man objectifies a woman's body by focusing on the sexual features instead of also noticing the woman's personality and feelings, but narcissistic mothers are decidedly guilty of denying their daughters' being by turning them into mere objects that suit their interactive styles and demands.

The difference with narcissistic parenting is that everything centers around the need for control. Sons are often excluded from the mother's interaction with their sisters. Some narcissistic mothers idealize their sons and place pressure on them to achieve and become successful. Most narcissistic maternal envy is directed toward their sons' female partners who are perceived as a threat.

On the other hand, the mother may treat the daughter more like a confidante. The relationship can become an enmeshed dynamic where all boundaries are ignored. She may even be envious of the daughter's appearance and always try to perfect or compare it to her own. The narcissistic mother's goal is to prevent the daughter from establishing closeness with other family members. I remember how the constant bombardment of inappropriate sexual secrets between my mother and father prevented me from forming a close connection with my father until his dying day. During these one-sided 'conversations,' she always made me aware of his sexual deviancy and how much it contributed to her profound distress. Eventually, my sister and I established a boundary and told my mother that we refused to listen to the secrets any longer. When she tries to share them, we deliberately ignore her and change the topic of conversation.

The hypercritical characteristic of narcissistic mothers enhances favoritism. Because of the objectification of each child in the family dynamic, various roles are attributed to the different children. Let's look at some ways of objectification.

The Golden Child

The golden child is the crown princess of the family. She brings glory to the family, she becomes an object that the family values, and this elevates the narcissistic grandiosity of the parent. The golden child receives better and more attention, validation, time, and resources. She becomes an extension of the parent but also a source of narcissistic supply, especially when the parent perceives the child as a reflection of themself. This favored child becomes the "specially anointed" child.

Sometimes the golden child shows that she deserves this special treatment, but other times she experiences it as a challenge when relating with siblings. She can also experience a fall from grace when she disappoints the narcissistic parent in some way or when she engages too closely with other siblings, thus threatening the narcissistic mother. The position can cause conflicting relational and emotional disturbances within the child's psyche.

The golden child is at risk of becoming a grandiose and overindulgent narcissist as an adult. They often become entitled, dysregulated adults, expecting other people to treat them the same way as their narcissistic mother did. Because of this tendency, they do not have tolerance for others and consider themselves special. They may become successful adults, but the long-term burden of the golden child role may cause other siblings to distance themselves. The distancing of other siblings from the parent and golden child causes isolation. Sometimes, there is also competition between the narcissistic mother and the golden child, causing great discomfort to the daughter. The demands of the mother may lead to failure and disappointment in the golden child.

The golden child ends up with many feelings that form tremendous guilt. Because they sense the different treatment toward them, and because they then try to guide the narcissistic parent in relation to other siblings or the other parent, the golden child ends up in an unfair and uncomfortable 'envoy' position with special access to the narcissistic parent. It becomes a painful emotion to constantly feel guilty about being the chosen one. The estrangement and isolation from other family members increase distress. They become anxious adults, spending their lives making amends for what happened in their youth. They experience profound shame and constant self-devaluing reflection continues into adulthood.

They eventually feel stuck and obligated to manage the aging narcissistic parent. When this obligation becomes too overwhelming, they sometimes force the responsibility of the aging parent onto the scapegoat child. Escape is often difficult for the golden child because of the parent's 'hook' to hold them responsible. The hook can be money, illness, property, and so forth. The golden child is also often better resourced in the family setup because of the start-up benefits but later has difficulty establishing a balance with the siblings that is not based on guilt.

In some cases, the 'thoroughbred' golden child may become a successfully balanced and stronger adult who understands the toxic environment well, enabling them to support and foster siblings. For this scenario, it is crucial that the golden child should not gaslight, invalidate, or manipulate other siblings in order to have a healthy relationship with the others. It all remains an unwanted and heavy burden to bear. The most obvious path to recovery is to pay forward the gifts that come their way and avoid narcissistic tendencies themselves.

The Scapegoat Child

This is the one who gets blamed and ganged up against all the time regardless of their behavior or actions. The scapegoat child may even be the envy of everyone in the family (because of their outstanding drive for achievements, exceptional beauty, etc.) and hence receive constant criticism and isolation from the rest of the family. They are constantly gaslighted and emotionally abused. The narcissistic mother may even encourage abusive treatment toward the child. It is indeed a very wretched role for the child. It is also the most common role in the narcissistic family, and the child gets the continuous wrath and invalidation of the narcissistic parent.

The most significant mental health impacts in adult life are patterns of complex post-traumatic stress disorder (CPTSD), anxiety, major issues with low self-esteem, and generally not feeling good enough about themselves. The scapegoat child suffers emotionally from self-doubt and self-blame. They have difficulty with decision-making and maladaptive coping mechanisms with substances, food, shopping, or gambling. They end up becoming confused adults, alienated from life, and suffering from constant grief.

Relationship issues are rife and the scapegoat child continues to subconsciously choose partners who replicate the narcissistic parent's invalidation cycle. They struggle to fully pursue educational and career goals in life, and they are always hearing their parent's voices saying, for example, "Who do you think you are?" or, "Do you really think you can do this?"

The scapegoat child continues the eternally dysfunctional relationship-chasing throughout life, more than the invisible child or the golden child. This child never believes that she deserves better and she believes that relationship issues are always her fault. She keeps on thinking she can change the narcissist and continuously suffers from physically and emotionally abusive relationships. She carries tremendous self-blame. She is constantly stuck and internalizes her emotions. She always feels responsible for her original family, never gets away from the manipulative toxicity, and never becomes a unique individual.

However, the dynamics of this narcissistic objectification do show some positive outcomes. The vast majority of scapegoat children can be highly empathic due to their learned behavior from childhood to always put others' needs first. But, when that scapegoat child one day discovers the wall of "having had enough," she is able to distance herself, cut ties completely, or set firm boundaries against the narcissistic parent (or intimate partner) effectively. After this realization, it is possible for the scapegoat child to reach awareness and full understanding of the narcissistic dynamics and they can henceforth spot a narcissist a mile away. They become the best "red flag detectors" in a room. Unfortunately, this understanding has to reach the child through the continuous journey of childhood pain and deep distress.

The Invisible Child

Fading into the woodwork is probably the most appropriate description for the invisible child. Even the scapegoat child gets attention, but the invisible child experiences neglect, she is never noticed and taken care of, and fades because of a complete lack of basic nurturing. She is the "headache child" for the narcissistic parent. She is an unwanted child. Her needs are overlooked, and she eventually internalizes the message that being quiet and invisible is the only way to get love. The invisible child becomes a burden in the family.

These children are generally quite introverted and do not want to be seen but they still do things to be noticed. As adults, they become attention-seeking individuals with a strong yearning to be seen and chronically feeling inferior. They often choose relationships later in life that echo the narcissistic parent dynamics. The ambiguity of choosing invisibility in situations, but having feelings of resentfulness about invisibility at the same time, creates confusion in self-regulation.

Being the invisible child is never a good setup for adulthood. They are never noticeable adults, they appear socially anxious, and show a limited ability to create safety. They internalize the message that their interests are not worthy, and they cannot execute visions and foster education to develop skills. In the workplace, they are often overlooked professionally and personally, and won't make deliberate attempts at success even when they are being noticed. They refuse to take personal risks, never achieve success, and become an afterthought.

The invisible child has one strong advantage over the other siblings. Their disappearance from a dysfunctional family system won't make an impact so they can make a clean break and create an opportunity for a fresh start to reinvent themselves despite the accompanying grief. They are able to become independent more quickly, and they show innovative ways of reinventing themselves. Apart from being strong survivalists, they also show a comfortable ability to be alone.

Narcissistic Control Tools

Two tactics that the narcissistic mother uses are triangulation and gaslighting. These traits often manifest in other relationships and work environments as well.

Triangulation

Narcissistic mothers thrive on drama and chaos. Triangulation is a favorite interpersonal device to manipulate the daughter. It gets forced on the child and the daughter does not consent to the psychological 'threesome' that the mother manipulates. The narcissistic mother uses the chaos that triangulation creates to control the situation and the people inside the situation.

Treating siblings differently through objectification generates the perfect environment for triangulation. It facilitates specific splitting and mistrust between all the family members because the narcissist is the only person who looks like the hero and who is ironically also the only person within the triangulation dynamics who is aware of the whole truth. The narcissistic mother will easily put down a particular sibling or even another parent to harness her power over the others. When, for example, drastic change takes place in a dysfunctional family system, the narcissistic mother perceives the change as a threat and employs triangulation to stabilize her own need for control. This may happen when a daughter introduces her future husband to the family.

Triangulation gives the maternal narcissist power. She compares her daughter with others to cultivate jealousy. It creates discomfort and imbalance with the siblings and ultimately enables the connection to become 'crowded.' Triangulation is a typical psychological device applied by toxic people. Narcissistic mothers enjoy the chaos where they are able to 'puppet' people around as they become objects to play with. It destabilizes the daughter who eventually becomes a suspicious and paranoid adult. The victimized daughter is often not aware of triangulation taking place and starts questioning herself. In its extreme form, the daughter starts to trust the narcissistic mother, who claims to hold the "true narrative," and thus gets brainwashed by her narcissistic lies. This will often result in infighting between siblings in order to win the favor of the narcissistic mother. Siblings end up inside an extremely unsettling scenario. The daughter at the mercy of a mother's triangulation may in future relationships be attracted to similar tendencies in a romantic partner because the partner initially appears charming and secretive when triangulation is employed to impress the 'victim.'

Why does triangulation take place in family dynamics? The primary reason is that it feeds the narcissistic parent by giving her invaluable control, validation, power, and attention. The most effective way to manage triangulation is when siblings unite together against the narcissistic parent. It is crucial to be able to identify the seeds of jealousy and recognize the narcissistic game in order to notice the pathological patterns and become a strong defensive circle to destabilize the narcissistic mother's triangulation. It requires tremendous strength to push past old wounds to break the toxic family dynamics. But it certainly can be done. The real power remains in the hands of the children.

Gaslighting

"Gaslighting is one of the most insidious forms of psychological abuse" (*Gaslighting Examples: The Most Covert Abuse Used by a Narcissistic Mother*, 2021). It is a volatile and manipulative form of emotional abuse with devastating consequences that make the child feel confused and disoriented. The scapegoat child is often the one who suffers most from gaslighting by the mother.

I remember as a child always feeling like I was doing everything wrong. I ended up living in a constant daze of confusion and my responses were monitored by the actions of significant others from various phases in my life. As a very young child, I used to mimic my mother's responses but as I became more aware of the deviancy of her behaviors, I started mimicking my sister's, or my father's, and later in life my partner's responses. It took years for my confidence to develop to such an extent that

I actually trusted my own intuitive response. As a result, I remained a quiet individual who hardly expressed any opinions or ideas and became anxious when I was forced to express myself. My mother constantly berated me for speaking too softly (which I did out of fear of being heard and for saying the wrong things) but then she would also liberally judge people who spoke too loudly!

Gaslighting is making someone else doubt their healthy sense of judgment, memory, and perception. The confusion creates tremendous cognitive dissonance. Children who are exposed to narcissistic parents' gaslighting techniques never develop healthy self-esteem or strong bonds of trust. They learn to never trust their own abilities and thoughts. The narcissistic mother does not care about what is actually right, she only cares about herself being right and she will confuse the daughter in every way to make herself feel powerful. Instead of supporting her daughter, she always makes the daughter feel worse about herself. Eventually, the daughter will try to do things simply to please the mother.

Sometimes the mother may shift the goalposts when she is being questioned. She may use phrases like, "That is not what really happened"; "Are you sure I said that?"; or "You are being too sensitive again, I was joking." It becomes a vicious cycle where the mother will never admit that she was wrong, or that she made a mistake, and eventually the daughter will be coerced into apologizing for the mother's mistake. In this way, the mother plays the victim and refuses acknowledgment of her mistakes. She may also project her own behaviors on the daughter.

Gaslighting takes place in four distinct ways: denial, misdirection, contradiction, and altering reality. The narcissistic mother creates psychological confusion by withholding or opposing crucial information and preventing the daughter from making an informed decision of her own. Until this day the phrase "I criticize you because I love you" makes me recoil. She may even question, overanalyze, or twist the daughter's decisions until the daughter doubts her own sanity. By being dismissive, saying something abusive, or ridiculing the daughter, the narcissistic mother will pretend as if nothing happened and even make the daughter believe that she is exaggerating. She will ultimately isolate the daughter from others who agree with her and contradict the mother.

Gaslighting features prominently in the enmeshed and authoritarian parenting styles. The 'gaslighted' child may find it challenging to communicate directly as an adult. Instead of speaking directly, they take the easy way of manipulating someone into doing what they want. In adult relationships, they may enhance drama to make the relationship feel 'normal' to them, or they may even lie about things that have no reason to be lied about. "You should have listened to your mother" or character statements like "You are a good daughter" all scream gaslighting! They may sound harmless but in essence, they negate the daughter's individuality. They smother.

The Effect of Maternal Narcissistic Manifestations

A mother is such an important developmental aspect of our lives that sets the course for future behavior. A narcissistic mother can set a highly destructive pathway for the daughter to become either overly anxious, have regulation issues, or risk becoming a narcissist herself. The daughter may also subconsciously navigate toward narcissistic relationships in her adult life. Some narcissists do not behave in cruel ways but their kindness and love are always conditional and come with terms. Their kindness carries an agenda. This results in serious attachment issues later in life. The daughter who becomes an extension of the mother will be an anxious child who always puts her own desires and needs aside for the mother. The narcissistic mother believes that she is the perfect mother and every mistake can be blamed on the daughter. The child learns to internalize this belief and continues blaming herself even when she is not at fault. The daughter often doesn't realize that there is something wrong and only becomes aware of the dysfunctional system much later in life, after all the damage is deeply rooted and requires intense therapy to make changes.

A few prominent outcomes of narcissistic parenting are:

- The daughter eventually feels selfish when she makes choices later in life, being conditioned by the narcissistic mother to always put the needs of others first. She feels selfish putting her own needs first. Indecision and guilt feelings cause tremendous hampering in her adult life.

- Imposter syndrome is a common result of internalized gaslighting. The daughter of a narcissistic mother may be conditioned to always believe that she is never good enough, she has little to offer, she doesn't deserve acknowledgment or praise, and she will always fail even after the mother's internal voice has been silenced.

- The daughter of a narcissistic mother finds it extremely frightening to enter relationships later in life that don't come with pre-conditions. She may also feel guilty when she leaves the narcissistic mother, or even when she puts boundaries in place to manage the mother's narcissism. For her, love and loyalty were always based on an agenda of conditions and manipulation and it became her 'normal.'

- She easily and almost chronically becomes the scapegoat in adult relationships and feels more comfortable taking the role of the accused in order to keep the peace. She had to take the blame as a child and continues to do so in other relationships as an adult.

- Narcissistic children always have to walk on eggshells with their mothers, who can emotionally explode at any time. Eventually, they are conditioned to become "insignificant in space"— they literally fade into the background to avoid drama.

- Daughters of narcissistic mothers subconsciously suffer from insecure attachment issues and they find it hard to liberate themselves from this. It is a result of the neglect, emotional absence, and manipulation that created insecurities of safety and trust with others. Some may become fiercely independent adults while others may become excessively clingy, demanding constant attention.

- Because many of these daughters have organized their lives around the happiness of their mother, they continue doing that in their adult lives with different relationships, always putting the needs and feelings of others before their own. Some even employ this in their career choices when they prefer to tend to others' needs in caring capacities.

- The positive outcome is that these daughters have strong resilience and a sense of compassion that they effectively apply to their future relationships and work environments.

Impact of Narcissistic Family Dynamics

The general impact of narcissistic family dynamics on the daughter is negative. Constant questions arise later in life like, "Why can I not win her over," or "Why is she always mad at me?" and these create malaise in adulthood. Commemorative holidays like Mother's Day can be a tense trigger point and cause anxiety in the daughter. The narcissistic mother will take inferior treatment personally and always find someone to blame. So, the daughter experiences a lifelong legacy of providing narcissistic supply to the "never satisfied" mother. Exhaustion eventually sets in while she continuously tries to appease her mother. The challenging situation increases isolation and the daughter becomes less trusting of others. Most daughters of narcissistic mothers feel a powerful sense of grief for having been robbed of a natural and deserving relationship with a mother.

Victim Entrapment

Narcissistic conditioning causes a life of entrapment for the victim. The daughter automatically inclines toward choosing codependent interactions in life with similar narcissistic tendencies, keeping her own feelings dependent on the narcissist's feelings while trying to keep everyone else constantly happy. A trauma-bonded guilt alliance develops throughout life in most of the daughter's world, which she never escapes from unless she makes a deliberate attempt to heal from the trauma.

Takeaway Guidelines

- The legacy of narcissistic family dynamics is miserable and they smother any progress.

- Narcissistic mothers tend to objectify their children as a means of control. The daughter can become the "golden child", the "scapegoat child" or the "invisible child", each with their own set of harrowing consequences.

- Two ways to control the daughter and retain a sense of power in the narcissist's mind are to use triangulation and gaslighting. Both create conflict and are intimidating forms of 'brainwashing.'

- Gaslighting in the form of denial, misdirection,

contradiction, and altering reality enables a confused and disoriented childhood.

- Prominent outcomes of the dysfunctional system have profound effects in the daughter's adult life and successive relations.

- The impact is mostly negative and exhaustive and creates a feeling of entrapment.

Calls to Action

- Focus on sibling unity as a defense mechanism against the narcissistic mother.

- Remind yourself of your strong resilience and your sense of compassion.

- Anticipate the narcissistic mother's dysfunctional coping tools and learn to manage them instead of allowing them to beat you.

Chapter 4

Protection From a Narcissistic Mother

In order to survive, you have to shrink yourself when near a narcissist.
–Jabeen et al.

My eyes are open now. How do I step away? It's not so much the traumatic stressor that caused the most havoc, it is the fact that the person I depended on to help me cope with the trauma was a non-existent entity in my most crucial developmental phase as a child. I had to make sense of the chaos alone. It was indescribable isolation. And it took many years to find release.

For the golden child and the scapegoat child, different experiences lead to contrasting conditioning and coping methods that have to be altered in order to step out of the damaging narcissistic cycle. The golden child may end up under tremendous pressure to perform and become successful while the scapegoat child may exhaust herself by pleasing people and not prioritizing her needs.

Boundaries

Establishing boundaries to create a healthy separation between you and the narcissistic mother is probably the most important step to take. Once the boundaries are established, you will be able to focus on improving your self-worth, and when your confidence levels have improved, you are able to manage the damage. Remember that setting boundaries implies immediately acting on the consequences, and every time when she crosses your limits.

Narcissistic mothers deny your selfhood. Your independence is a threat to them and this is the reason why they make all the boundaries fluid between you. They intimidate you to live in their shadow while having unrealistic expectations from you. This starts happening in childhood and continues into your adult life. Maybe she read your diaries, perhaps she never gave you the privacy you needed in a bathroom. Even oversharing her personal secrets with you was a violation of your privacy. Whether you were the golden child, the invisible child, or the scapegoat child, your boundaries were impacted dysfunctionally by your narcissistic mother. They make you believe that it's love when in reality it is not love. It's either possession that manifests as enmeshed boundaries, or its marginalization. The splitting of boundaries in this way results from the mother being unreasonably critical, always nit-picking, being judgmental, and making comparisons that shame and invalidate you. Her rejection of your success and achievements to fulfill her own selfish needs, desires, and dreams led to the diminishing of your individuality. Her contemptuously critical responses made you question your own boundaries while you subconsciously established dysfunctional ones.

To end this nauseating cycle of enmeshed immersion or abandonment (where you had no healthy framework of boundaries) you have to put up as well as maintain new, strong boundaries. It is crucial to remain vigilant and realistic about any manipulation and to work on your confidence because this is what she is trying to break down. Your own thoughts and feelings were never validated by your narcissistic mother who always put her own feelings first and kept you responsible for her emotions. To recover from this, it is crucial to maintain the boundaries that define and separate both her and your emotions and existence.

As a result of her narcissistic parenting style that diffused your healthy boundaries, it is necessary to manage anticipated conflict when you re-establish your separateness. She may show her jealousy when you show signs of individuation, separation, or independence. Here are some basic steps to take when implementing boundaries.

- Identify your boundary needs and act on them habitually, decisively, and quickly. If you can do this in writing, even better. State clearly what your limits are and what the consequences for crossing them would be.

- Manage your own personal agenda when uncomfortable questions are being asked. You may for example change the topic after giving a short answer to her question or you may even ignore the question. Take effective control of the discourse between you and your mother with this tactical step.

- Just leave. You do not always have to give an explanation for exiting an uncomfortable situation. You can even predetermine the allotted time you plan to spend with her. If she demands an explanation, you can say you are simply running late.

- Share only essential information. Remember that the more personal details the narcissistic mother has, the more she manipulates you. Control the amount and type of details that you do share with her. Stand your ground when she criticizes you by saying something like "Thank you, I will remember your advice" and then move on.

- By calling her out, you are making her aware of your boundary, and remember that her response is irrelevant. If you have said to her that you will leave when she interrupts you, follow through after telling her that she interrupted you. Do this every time she does this to you.

You deserve to be treated respectfully and she has to know this.

Taking Back Power

Once the boundaries are in place and you are able to maintain them, the focus can shift to your self-esteem. A narcissistic mother can be a formidable challenge, and because she simply refuses to acknowledge her shortcomings and refuses to make any changes to herself, the management of the relationship depends on your strength and awareness.

A narcissistic mother does not treat you as a human being.

Her objectification of you is depriving you of your sense of individuality. Her abuse of your confidence with her entitled behavior, and in some cases grandiose behavior, inhibits your healthy development and keeps the focus firmly rooted on herself and her own needs. Your needs always come second and sometimes have to be ignored or hidden and sometimes completely aborted. Taking back your power as an individual requires a deliberate focus on developing your sense of self.

Her constant negative comparisons have a profound impact on your self-esteem. She often uses gaslighting to make you doubt your own reality and to break your sense of self-worth down. It is one of the cruelest forms of emotional abuse that any person can inflict on another because it makes you believe that you are going crazy. If it is coming from a primary caregiver, it makes the psychological damage even worse. It's an easy way out for the narcissist because she doesn't have to change herself, she only has to blame and convince you that you are wrong. So, she remains the perfect example that you can never become no matter how hard you try. If she doesn't corrupt you to believe that she is the image of perfection, she will compare you to others. The goal is to make you look and feel inferior. It is important to learn to trust your own concept of reality and to learn to trust that your perceptions are not as distorted as she would like you to believe. Humans make mistakes but humans also remember, and if you really doubt yourself, it makes sense to ask a trusted friend to check in and give honest feedback.

Your narcissistic mother always makes you aware that she is the mother at the expense of your being alive. She is making you less 'human.' It is possible to take back your power when you realize that you are not a trophy offspring, you are a person with a heart. End the cycle of boosting her already inflated ego and downplaying your own sense of self.

Narcissistic abuse eventually creates existential tiredness from constant condemnation. Taking a nap or improving your sleep patterns simply does not solve the tiredness. Fatigue robs you of hope. The daily struggles with your circumstances become a confusing challenge and leave you emotionally exhausted. To protect yourself from your narcissistic mother, you have to step away from the toxic behavior and not expect sympathy from her. If you tell her you are tired, she may gaslight and invalidate you, so keep a realistic daily pace and expectations, and stop competing with others who appear to do more than you.

The silent treatment is a key narcissistic weapon to manipulate, punish, and violate you until you blame yourself. It's basically a tantrum! She is showing her lack of interpersonal skills and it is a miserable and dramatic experience. It is actually easier to argue. The best medicine is to 'outstare' her dramatic show, do not blame yourself, and give the treatment back to her! It is an unhealthy red flag relationship dynamic and once you are aware of its dysfunctional nature, you can avoid manipulative engagement.

As the scapegoat child, you were bombarded with criticism and an onslaught of fault-finding. To break the cycle, it is important to understand that you were not worthy of the humiliation that you received, it certainly was not normal and you recover once you stop believing that you deserved what happened to you. Very often in scapegoat child family dynamics, the narcissistic mother coerces the other members to gang up against one child in order to make her feel powerful and in control. The siblings (sometimes it also includes another parent) go along with this in order to gain her approval and to avoid her emotional outbursts of anger. Her sadistic sense of feeling powerful over your vulnerabilities feeds her narcissistic tendencies. To show your suffering to her invites her to do more harm. Her demented need for power and control does not perceive your suffering as a reason to stop tormenting you. In fact, she blames you constantly in order to obtain a false sense of superiority that she is unaware of. It takes your firm awareness of the reasons why she blames you to break the cycle and not allow her the satisfaction of breaking you down anymore.

You do not have to be someone else's emotional 'punch bag' all the time. Life is worth living separately from being your narcissistic mother's 'scapegoat' who always operates on terms of what you "should not be." You do have the right to 'be'! Identify the difference between 'attachment' and 'abuse.' Stop hiding away your good qualities, attributes, and hidden talents, because your self-worth is important. Always having distorted self-defeating beliefs about yourself can lead to exhaustion, maladaptive functioning, and in extreme cases to body dysmorphic disorder (BDD), the phenomenon where a person distorts the realities about their appearance, believing that they are 'disgusting.' It's exhausting to always live in a sense of looming dread, like "I am always one mistake away from complete ruin" (Reid, 2019). Being constantly terrorized as a child by a narcissistic mother and other siblings made you believe that the smallest wrong move will result in something awfully final and there is no escape from the ensuing wrath. To recover from this, you have to realize that you are not defective. You have to understand that mistakes are made and are part of the normal cycle of life, and we all have the ability to recover from our mistakes.

For the golden child, taking back power requires a different set of habits. The golden child who grew up may find in adult life that she worships authority, and sometimes unjustly enforces and enables authority in order to maintain her needs for acknowledgment. (This also manifests in relational and career environments.) To break this cycle, you have to break off the habit of pleasing your mother. Your unrealistic fear of failure results from your being objectified. Your narcissistic mother ignored your individual character (and identity) while your achievements were always praised. So as an adult, you keep searching for approval and you endlessly wait for your mother's acknowledgment. You were subconsciously conditioned to be scared of failure. Your fear of being outperformed by others, and living in constant competition, becomes challenging. It is important to stop labeling yourself as the "good person" which can become an exhausting habit. Being a flawed human being is the general norm and it's acceptable!

Many daughters of narcissistic mothers have inflated feelings of inadequacy. This was mostly enabled by the narcissistic mother who coerced you to perform and achieve in order to meet her selfish standards and needs. To recover from this is important to understand that it is not your status or skills or talents that make you worthy of being human. Cease chasing the illusion of what your mother created, and focus instead on the reality of your human side, beautiful flaws and all.

Enjoy your own company, you do not always have to keep performing to achieve. Start enjoying your free time and make the necessary adjustments to your perception of productivity requirements.

Disengagement

Disengaging may be the most challenging step in the process to protect yourself from your narcissistic mother because she perceives your disobedience or deviation from engagement as a threat. Your lack of complete attention becomes menacing and she blames you for it. However, it is important to understand that it is actually her desire to control you and she becomes irate when she loses control. But the reality is that you may only be able to see the real damage once you have disengaged yourself from her toxic environment.

Some narcissistic mothers expect their children to take care of them in various ways (financially, physically, emotionally, or psychologically) and thus enforce their way to maintain control and dependency or codependency while denying your separateness from them. Although it is a noble endeavor to care for aging parents, it is unhealthy when this care is a result of demanding manipulation from the parent. It is thus important to determine if your mother is transferring her narcissistic expectations to you or if your care is genuine and healthy. A good indicator is when the caring comes with unreasonable sacrifices while your personal priorities and needs are ignored or neglected. This situation easily manifests as a codependent one where the daughter ends up enabling the mother's weakness. A codependent relationship is appropriately described by professor of psychology Shawn Burn as "one person's help supports (enables) the other's underachievement, irresponsibility, immaturity, addiction, procrastination, or poor mental or physical health" (Ni, 2016).

Living a life of disturbing codependency is a pattern of cyclic toxicity and narcissistic engagement with others. The golden child often struggles with codependency after being conditioned to enable the narcissistic mother's needs. She expects praise from the mother and when the approval does not happen, maternal anger ensues or the mother causes trouble. The conditioning feeds the endless cycle of enabling in different environments. Approval leads to mutual exploitation or collaboration when someone else (e.g., in work or relational environment) recognizes the golden child's talents and abilities, praises the golden child, and gives more opportunities and attention, which leads to the golden child conforming to expectations of the enabler. "The golden child wears a metaphorical set of handcuffs, in that, they are stuck in performance" (Brian, 2022).

The scapegoat child, on the other hand, becomes an

agreeable person who always complies with others' expectations. This results from a fear of abandonment or being exiled from the family and she learns to control her impulses, feelings, and reactions in order to avoid an onslaught of anger, conflict, emotional outbursts, or disagreement. Living with a chronic sense of feeling discomfort in your own skin, and never being able to relax, becomes exhausting. To recover from this dysfunctional interaction and disengage from the toxic maternal environment requires confidence. Rebuilding your confidence starts with realizing that not everyone will think hateful things of you when you disagree with them, only your narcissistic mother did! The focus of your recovery is not on how others perceive you, it's rather that there are people who think well of you and that others may welcome your disagreement. Harness the positive reinforcement, be brave, be bold, and speak up!

The primary goal of disengagement is to create separateness. In some cases, it may not be possible to make a clean cut with the narcissistic mother and you can opt for a low-contact disengagement scenario. This requires some deliberate steps to make it work.

- Design a plan of limited contact, write it down, give her a copy, and stick to it.

- Discuss the rules with her and be prepared for the guilt trip that she may want to force on you for making these changes. Stick to a respectful explanation without emotion.

- Inform and include intimate family members who will understand her responses in your plan. Make them aware of your decision.

- When you do interact with her after these arrangements, stick to neutral topics of discussion. Do not allow her to venture onto personal and sensitive terrain.

- Make time and maintain your alone time, allowing yourself to recover after interaction with her. Do not let her take this valuable time away from you. You deserve to focus on your own needs as well.

- Stay calm, do not challenge her, and change confrontational topics. When she sees that her confrontational topics do not affect you, she may stop them altogether over time.

- Have a support network ready who will understand your decision and encourage you to maintain it.

- Be specific with your boundaries. Use direct words like "If you mention my father's infidelity again, I will change the topic" or "If you call me that name again, I will hang up the phone."

- Give her a list of the boundaries and their resulting consequences that you will enforce. Don't allow her to manipulate you.

- Be unavailable sometimes. She will start to realize that she is not the sole focus of your existence. It's easy to say that "I am busy at work."

- When you do not react emotionally, you take the puppet master's toys away and she loses her power. Stay calm, no matter what happens. Take control.

- Engaging with her in public places may help to manage all the above. She does not want to appear bad in front of others.

- Don't give her the ammunition of your intentions and personal plans. She will simply undermine them.

- Avoid her manipulative tactics by remaining a "gray rock" as Dr. Ramani suggests. Do not defend yourself, nor explain yourself. Simply give answers that are unemotional and neutral.

- Don't wait for her approval, it will never happen. Live your life and liberate yourself from this desire.

- Observe her instead of engaging with her behavior, by detaching yourself emotionally from her. This is a natural disengagement tactic and it relieves the tension.

- There is nothing unhealthy about being independent and taking a physical break from your narcissistic mother for an extended period.

- Make it a habit to walk away from confrontation with her, this will immediately disarm her and encourage her to find alternative tactics for engagement.

- Find therapy to hold you and guide you through his process. You do not have to fight her alone.

General Guidelines

Our narcissistic mothers have an endless supply of tactics to manipulate and invalidate us. Whenever they feel threatened, they pull them out relentlessly and aim them at our most vulnerable spots. While you are slowly taking back your power after implementing secure boundaries and managing your engagement with her, be conscious of some of the following manipulation tools that she may use. It is also useful to be aware of these in other areas of your life when you engage in a toxic work environment, or in a close relationship, and even with your own children who may trigger conditioned responses from you.

Managing Triggers

Your narcissistic mother has an unflagging sense of your vulnerabilities and she knows how to trigger them to get a specific reaction from you. A repetitive history of conditioned reactions to triggers may predict your current behavior and disrupt new relationships in many environments. The following steps may be useful to manage triggers.

- Identify the triggers: To regain control of situations in your life, know and understand the things that trigger your responses.

- Coping plan: Design a plan to implement and regulate in response to the triggers.

- Share: Tell your significant others about your coping mechanisms and plans. Make them aware of the anticipated responses when triggers should happen. Ask for their support. Some daughters of narcissistic mothers have difficulty asking for help, it's useful to cultivate the habit of trusting specific people that you know will understand and support you. Engage in direct and honest communication with them. You are allowed to be vulnerable with people you can trust.

- Coping tools: Continue using them regularly as a habit-forming tool to manage triggers. Focus on using calming techniques. I have found coping tools that focus on breathing like yoga, meditation, shiatsu, etc. the most efficient. Find one or two that relieves your emotional response the most effectively, and routinely practice them.

An example of a healthy coping plan can be a time-out schedule once you identify the trigger. If you forewarn your significant others that you will leave the room for ten minutes after being triggered to do a calming meditation and then return, they will not be alarmed. You may even return after ten minutes to say that you need more time. In this way, you manage your triggers and keep your loved ones informed and alleviate additional anxiety. In extreme situations where anxiety takes control (like with unexpected panic attacks), they will be able to support you by reminding you of your chosen coping plan.

Responding to Narcissistic Mothers

It is necessary to know that a personality usually doesn't change much over its lifespan. For narcissists, it is generally impossible because they lack an understanding of how their tendencies affect you, so a powerful tool in the hands of the narcissistic victim is to focus on behavior because this can be prevented or adjusted. Narcissistic communication causes the damage. By managing their communication with your reflective responses (pause and think before you respond) the waiting period provides time to analyze and engage intelligently. With time it may even be possible to make a narcissistic mother aware of this type of reflective communication and engage her cooperation. Finding the right way to communicate with her will provide guaranteed relief from conflict situations as well as strengthen your confidence.

Anger Management

Manage her anger and maternal rage. Your narcissistic mother's emotional outbursts were the primary cause of your reactive or depressive responses. Learning to regulate uncomfortable and overwhelming emotions is crucial to protecting yourself. Managing her narcissistic rage means having to focus on the natural separation that is supposed to take place as you mature into adulthood. Your narcissistic mother sees you as an extension of herself, and when you reach maturity that naturally entails a separation from her, she feels threatened and tries to pull you back. Narcissistic mothers often intrude into your marriage and even your private sexual life. If you put up resistance to this, she may attack your husband or partner in order to achieve her goal of garnering you back into her sphere. An understanding of her reasons behind the anger is crucial to diffuse emotions. Five easy to diffuse aggressive situations are:

- Remind her that you are both in the situation together. Don't use 'I' or 'you' when conversing with her because she may perceive it as blame and this will enrage her more. You may think that you are simply defending yourself but she certainly does not.

- Any perceived judgment or criticism toward her is seen as a threat. Rather emphasize the results of her anger and try to improve the discourse. Do not tell her that she is wrong. She will never believe you.

- Empathy may help to calm her down. She cannot show empathy so you will have to show it for both of you.

- Use the bait of distraction. Narcissists like to talk about themselves and if you change the conversation to a personal topic about her, she may forget about her rage.

- Remember that she will do anything to remind you of your shortcomings and past mistakes to get a reaction from you. Don't show the hurt, instead, stay calm and do not show a reaction. Do not take the bait!

Defying Projecting and Violations

To manage the narcissist's projecting, condescending, or intrusive behavior requires an understanding of the interaction between the narcissist and your conditioned low self-esteem. A daughter with low confidence levels tends to 'introject' the projection until she believes it to be true. As a result of this, feelings of shame arise and inter-relational issues evolve. Your weakness sends a message to the narcissistic mother who made the projection that she has a right and power over your confidence. Highly empathic people are more susceptible to projection. If you add weakened boundaries to low self-esteem, you are doomed for disaster. A highly valuable tool to protect yourself against violation is to recognize the abuser's defense mechanism when she is unconsciously showing her own weakness, for example, shame by shaming you. When you understand that she is projecting her weakness on you, then you find empathy which in turn reinforces your self-esteem. It is thus important to learn to disarm your inner critic as the first option of defense against a narcissistic abuser. Don't argue, simply confirm your disagreement and walk away.

Managing Maternal Obsessions

Manage your obsessions with an abusive mother whether the abuse is excessive gifting from her, emotional manipulation, nurturing demands, or financial expectations. Especially the golden child has to take deliberate steps to distance herself from becoming entangled and trapped in the needs of the mother. I remember how I watched as an outsider how my mother manipulated my father (and after he passed away, she switched to my sister) to do everything for her as if she was incapable of taking care of her own needs and obligations. She simply still refuses to take responsibility for managing her own affairs and I still see my sister being clamped around without release.

Managing Narcissistic Lying

Narcissists believe they deserve to lie and they justify their lying by saying it is necessary. Eventually, the lie feels like the truth to them, they perceive it as technically correct and ignore the feeling that accompanies the act. An efficient way to manage the lies is to divert the narcissistic mother to listening instead of talking. You can change the topic, ignore her comment, and engage the narcissistic mother in a new conversation by using softening phrases like "I mean this in a friendly way"; "I hope this makes sense"; and "What do you think of this?" It's not what you say, it's how you say it.

Takeaway Guidelines

- Three important steps to protect yourself are to firstly understand what happened, secondly put a distance between you and the narcissistic mother, and lastly, defy the conditioned beliefs that she imposed on you.

- Implementing and maintaining boundaries, taking back your power, and disengaging from the toxic environment determine your healing journey.

- Further assistance comes from managing triggers, communicative responses, invalidation, violation and projection, maternal obsessions, and focusing on maternal lying and anger management.

Calls to Action

- Establish at least one reliable connection to whom you can go for advice and guidance when you feel vulnerable.

- Give up the quest of trying to prove your mother wrong.

- Change your beliefs, debunk the myths you were forced to believe, do not only acknowledge them, but also challenge them.

- Take credit for your strengths, your own needs are as important as others' needs.

Chapter 5

Avoiding Toxic Relationships

"I'm unlovable" became a belief that many of us took into our adult relationships.

–Irina

Narcissistic mothers often use withholding of love as a form of punishment. It can manifest as silent treatment and in extreme cases complete abandonment. Your mother made you aware that your behavior was the primary reason for her unhappiness. In addition to this, she invalidated your viewpoints and your individuality. She broke down any healthy boundaries, showed no empathy when you needed her, and she manipulated you to believe that you have no worth and can give no value to any connection. Now you bring this to your other relationships in adult life. The consequences are devastating.

Manifestations and Symptoms of Victimization

The victimized daughter's coping methods overlap in various adult relationships. She brings her habits into friendships, when raising her own children, and most profoundly in intimate romantic relationships because the close nature of these relationships triggers many memories and coping strategies. She displays the subconscious intuitive patterns in all her connections and then questions her already low self-esteem by internalizing others' responses. She constantly feels unheard, has trouble saying 'no' and also difficulty with being told 'no', has trouble expressing herself, and displays a compulsive behavior to "make herself heard."

She mostly struggles with issues around anger, trust, control, and security. Her close relationships are short-lived, filled with conflict and emotion, and show instability and insecurity. The irony is that she usually craves to be loved but she is constantly self-sabotaging at the same time, ending up in a typical disjunction of an abused daughter who is always suffocating her connections. The push-and-pull phenomenon is a result of insecurity and low self-esteem. It is conditioned by a maternal narcissistic relationship that never allowed her to establish healthy boundaries and limits in a close connection. The scapegoat child easily becomes the "dumping place" for someone else's abuse and betrayal. The invisible child ventures into unhealthy connections because she does not see herself as worthy of love. The golden child may end up shaming herself for attempts at autonomy outside her mother's sphere of demands. She may also never be able to release the entrapment of the mother's clamping as she struggles to let go.

Because our romantic relationships are so closely linked to a similar level of intimacy that we yearned for as a child, the psychological phenomenon of "repetition compulsion" (like a narcissistic repetition) is a very real possibility in victimized adult relationships. All the partners that we date become our narcissistic mother and we never seem to escape the abusive trap. Why do we subconsciously tend to steer toward something that we know is not good for us? Why do we end up in these abusive relationships later in life and often return to them despite the knowledge that they are harmful? The answer is simple—because it is familiar to you. Researchers call this a legacy of maternal/paternal self-absorption that immortalizes the damage.

Victims of abuse display many manifestations, depending on the intensity level, the kind of abuse, and also the duration of the abuse. Sexual abuse (for example) manifests differently and it is important to regulate the symptoms with therapeutic guidance on an individual basis. Some children may become abusive adults in order to try and repair their dysfunctional childhood memory. Others may repetitively become involved in abusive relationships since these are their conditioned framework models. In this way, negative relationships become your new normal.

The first step to recovery from an abusive romantic relationship is leaving the narcissistic abuser. The second step is to stay away, and it is this step that presents more difficulty for the abused child when she matures. As a child who could not leave her parent, and as a child who came to identify her nurturer as the one who also hurts her, she cannot make this distinction and the separation comes with extreme and deliberate effort. It is helpful to have a trusted friend or counselor who can help you through his process. My trusted sister helped me to regain my independence after a painful break-up by making me text her (instead of my narcissistic ex-partner) every time when I felt compelled to make contact with him.

Physical —Constantly Feeling on Alert

Research has found that the brain and the body remember pain long after it has ceased. Chronic pain can thus develop long after the damage has gone because the body still registers the memory. Similarly, any emotional pain that is not processed properly will linger in the body because the tension tends to take over the nervous system and cause chronic physical pain in the body. Emotional and physical pain may even enable one another in a cyclic pattern if they are not being processed. It has become evident that an abusive past teaches the body to stay in a hypervigilant state of alertness to protect itself and remain in a constant "survival mode."

The bodily overproduction of stress hormones (like adrenaline and cortisol) affects your pain levels and immune system. The resulting fluctuations in blood pressure and heart rate eventually damage the body's organs, joints, and adrenal glands. Liver issues may develop, not only from substance abuse but also from increased stress levels. You may be startled easily. The symptomatic responses to an abusive past are extremely varied and each person responds differently. When you suffered an injury at the hand of a physically abusive parent (for example a broken limb) the memory of that injury may remain despite the fact that the injury healed over time. So, past physical abuse will linger in the present and cause chronic strain. It becomes a physical reminder of the abuse and emotional impact on your being, fueling the emotional reminder of a physical injury from the damaging past.

The act of "avoiding life" by limiting social interaction and physical activities can be the cause of back pain, joint pain, and migraines as your muscles respond to refraining from exercise. Our bodies are intelligent, and even when they simply hold tension because they experience a sense of something 'wrong' without knowing the cause, they may respond with chronic pain. We know now that the brain and the body are connected in ways that we do not always understand, but bodily pains should make us aware that there may be some unresolved trauma that we need to address. They are sending out alert signs to us and we need to listen to them. Digestive issues, allergic reactions, irritable bowel syndrome (IBS), and eating disorders are mostly established psychologically.

Psychological—Stuck in Your Skin

The mind finds a way to deal with excessive and repetitive trauma by distancing or detaching itself from the trigger/s. (This is a natural process resulting from continuous trauma that is discussed in detail in Chapter 7 when we look at CPTSD). The process is called dissociation and though it may appear to bring relief, it actually does not help. It remains a very unhealthy coping mechanism. The brain simply distances the memory, distressing thoughts, and feelings from the experience but the unresolved trauma remains while subconsciously causing mayhem under your skin. Abused individuals often suffer from insomnia, depression, panic attacks, and the list goes on. A general feeling of not feeling comfortable in your skin may remain stuck for years.

In extreme scenarios, the brain may even create memory loss, memory distortion, or gaps in memory that can become extremely confusing and affect your daily functioning. Even though your brain is trying to help you cope with the stress, you are actually not coping, and the awareness of this triggers more anxiety. Depersonalization-derealization disorder is symptomatic of trauma and intense stress. It manifests as numbness or fogginess, like a feeling of being "outside yourself" and an awareness of a detachment from the world, a sense of being disconnected from yourself. It almost feels like looking at yourself from an elevated position. In extreme situations, it may even have a paralyzing effect on the body. The sense of detachment from one's body or mental processes can be extremely distressing. Some patients experience bodily distortions like a sense of their arms being shrunken or enlarged. It can be a frightening experience when it makes you feel like you are losing control, but in many ways, the dissociation helps you to recover before you react to a specific trigger. It happens subconsciously as the brain responds internally to the trigger, not intentionally. The brain is trying to cope with the intensity of the traumatic memories.

In some cases, repetitive and unhealthy habits to cope with stress levels and to block out painful memories (like drinking, abusing drugs, or smoking excessively) eventually take their toll on your physical health by causing inflammation. (Researchers call this pain-producing coping behavior.) The unhealthy coping styles and mechanisms can only be managed when the individual starts addressing her vulnerability in exchange for a healthier vulnerability. Rebuilding self-esteem, acquiring higher confidence levels, and learning to trust your intuition are the building blocks for recovering from abusive connections.

Relational—Always Feeling Defective

"Because it is tied to early development, trauma in childhood gets imprinted in the brain and changes the ability to respond to stress and to have healthy relationships" (Robins, 2020). Narcissistic mothers damage relationships with their daughters. They do not repair them. The daughter has to cope with her overload of confusion and emotional disturbances on her own. Constant shaming from the mother further enables the disintegration of a healthy self-concept and we end up seeing ourselves as defected human beings. If we cannot love ourselves, how are we supposed to love another person? This fragmented and dissociative self attracts dysfunctional connections and also hijacks every other relationship in our lives. So, the link between the past and the present forever presents itself and merges into false and other abusive realities. Raising our own children with the constant fear of making the same mistakes, or subconsciously 'mothering' our children like we were 'mothered', or not being a good mother become another daunting and overwhelming chapter in our lives. This is why separation from the past trauma is the key to recovery.

The fear of letting people down, trust issues, constant abandonment issues, and always having your value measured against the series of successes or failures that you presented, prepared you for the next chapter of unhealthy toxic intimate relationships. The golden child interprets interaction in various environments as a reflection of their achievements and successes. If their partner does not validate this with responses of praise and acknowledgment, they react emotionally. A relationship is viewed as a transaction and they base their behavioral responses on this perspective. The invisible child and the scapegoat child bring other dimensions to their adult relationships and ultimately also remain trapped in the narcissistic abuse spiral unless they deliberately make the separation and implement change.

Managing Attraction

Attachment theory defines a child's healthy development of a sense of self by interpreting the mother's facial responses. Narcissistic daughters always yearn to be seen because their mothers never saw them for who they are. In some cases, they completely ignored them, which led to serious abandonment issues in succeeding relationships. This distorted concept of attachment shows in their attraction styles and how they manage other relationships. It manifests in their career environments and permeates their social functioning.

Daughters who suffered from maternal narcissistic abuse have extreme difficulty with stability and quality in their intimate adult relationships. Everything inside a close relationship triggers dysfunctional coping methods, habits, misconceptions, and interpretations. Close relationships become an exhausting challenge (for both parties) of always being defensive, hypervigilant, and overly self-critical. The daughter's coping mechanisms were her survival tools and she habitually applied them to new scenarios, only to subconsciously validate the same scenario.

Neglecting your physical self, organizing your life around other people's perceived needs, making other people happy at your own expense, and sacrificing your own interests to improve another person's discontent becomes an exhausting daily habit. The victimized daughter always had to manage situations with disapproval, conflict, and invalid criticism and she learned to put herself second in order to maintain the peace. This conditioning does not foster healthy attachment in adult relationships.

Intimate Relationships

You are too emotional, or too sensitive, or too dramatic, or too high-maintenance, or anything with the adjective 'too' attached to it, makes me cringe. This is the narcissist's favorite way of invalidating your emotions and keeping you quiet. They deflect the abuse back at you and force you into submission. Why does this keep happening and why can't we escape from it? One reason is that the narcissist exploits our fears and vulnerabilities, and unless we understand their functioning, we remain trapped in self-hate and disgust. They continue their abuse and the cycle never ends. Another reason is that we are conditioned to remain close and intimate with the abuser. We try to help them and rescue them from their own wounds and when they perceive this empathy as a threat, they start to withdraw, leaving us with feelings of rejection, insecurities, and deeply sad. The more we try to "win them back" the more we suffocate the relationship and an unhealthy spiral of attraction and defense develops. In extreme cases, our actions and responses may become vengeful and destructive, and we end up questioning our sanity in highly tumultuous and unstable circumstances. A narcissistic partner is highly aware of this attachment insecurity and knows how to feed it.

Daughters of narcissistic mothers often display these traits of clinginess or opposing distancing in relationships and they never find harmony but instead gather a list of short-lived romantic relationships filled with conflict. We tend to close out the people whom we love the most simply because we have a deep sense of feeling unsafe in any intimate environment. We were never able to develop a healthy sense of trust because our trusted 'carer' was also the main person who hurt us. To amplify the struggle, we always face emotional dysregulation when we are faced with conflict, criticism, or disapproval. It's a tough trap to escape. It can be overwhelming and exhausting. Your narcissistic mother primed you. The choice is yours to stay there or to let go.

Toxic Career Choices, Work Environments, and Coworkers

Apart from spending a large part of our adult lives interacting with others on an intimate level, we spend most of our time in some kind of work environment where we are forced to interact in prescribed ways. Our workplaces come with rules, demands, requirements, expectations, and boundaries that may be daunting for the daughter of a narcissist. We are so conditioned to behave ourselves in the ways that our mothers demanded from us that we may misinterpret any sign that triggers a memory. Each objectified child will respond in different ways to this forced interaction. We end up showing a subconscious attraction to toxic career environments and career choices that ultimately impact and enable our conditioned responses.

The invisible child grew up believing that she makes no impact, that she doesn't matter, and in many cases, this leads to patterns of procrastination and postponement of a healthy career path. Her fear-driven concept robs her of success and she often overcompensates by being 'nice' and compliant. She avoids conflict situations and never rocks the boat.

The scapegoat child has been conditioned that she is always wrong and should take the blame for everything. To satisfy her mother and in an attempt to harness her approval, she strove for perfection. These children end up in the work environment driven by compulsive habits and an endless chase of perfectionism that inhibit their activities and prevent them from obtaining success. They tend to stall on the ladder. They often choose career paths in the compassion industry like teaching, nursing, or psychiatry.

The golden child in the work environment is almost impossible to work with because she grew up believing that she is special and talented. These children constantly received praise from the parents, resulting in entitlement issues and consequently expecting constant promotion and instant recognition in the work environment. If it doesn't happen and they discover that the work environment does not solely focus on them, they end up losing interest in their job, they work poorly, or exhibit teamwork issues as they self-sabotage. They also overestimate their abilities since the narcissistic mother made them believe that they were semi-superhuman, so they believe that their abilities are superior to others. They find it challenging to hear from a manager that they are not perfect, although hearing this from coworkers does not seem to impact them as much.

These are generalizations of objectification. In many instances the child of a narcissistic mother may manifest different symptoms; some may even exhibit narcissistic traits in the work environment themselves. But showing significant impairments with "life tasks" (e.g., holding a job, stability with housing, financial management, achievement in relational or academic and professional scenarios, developmental goals, and goal setting) remain more challenging for children of narcissistic parents.

Managing Toxic Coworkers and Work Environments

Many work environments come with a variety of personalities and for the victimized daughter of a narcissistic mother, exposure to emotional abuse at work presents difficulty. Narcissistic abuse in these environments is often unnoticed and happens covertly. It varies from shaming someone, making someone feel guilty, or intimidating a person. It can be disguised as not having a superior listening to your valid concerns or being given false hopes and promises that never materialize. For an abused individual, this does not only affect her capabilities at work to complete tasks and perform well but it cuts into deep emotional trauma and affects her self-esteem. In many scenarios, a person may not be able to set boundaries or leave the work environment which sets her up for prolonged emotional scarring. The ideal situation is to detach and separate from the narcissistic environment, reframe one's concept of requirements and needs, implement boundaries and limits, or ultimately remove oneself completely from the toxic workplace—if this is possible!

Takeaway Guidelines

- Your mother's lack of empathy and boundaries, dysfunctional loving, manipulation, abandonment, punishment, and invalidation created your low self-esteem that you exhibit in other adulthood relations.

- The victimized symptoms manifest physically and psychologically in intimate relationships, work environments, friendships, and in your own maternal capacity with your children—repeating and enabling toxic environments.

- Your fears and senseless feelings of deficiency show themselves in your attachment style.

Calls to Action

- Focus on recreating your self-esteem and self-worth. Your journey depends on your strength.

- Detach from toxic relationships and work environments if possible.

- If you cannot disengage, at least make the deliberate choice to manage them and stick to your plan.

- You make the choices.

Chapter 6

Re-mothering the Daughter

A person's authentic nature is a series of shifting, variegated planes that establish themselves as he relates to different people; it is created by and appears within the framework of his interpersonal relationships.
–Philip K. Dick

This quote by the science-fiction writer Philip K. Dick emphasizes the fallacy of static relations and personality. We can disprove the myth that a person has a fixed personality throughout their lives. Understanding our human side implies an understanding of character. Many thinkers from cross-disciplinary fields theorize that a person's character is fluid and it responds to the individual's particular environmental context. Our personalities do not stay static throughout our lives, we have the ability to mold them. This gives me hope.

The challenge arises after narcissistic childhood, when the daughter's personality manifests the developmental and archetypal effects of narcissistic abuse. Anticipatory angst, constantly expecting blame and accusations, feelings of inadequacy, fear of failure, harboring disappointment and rage, emotional emptiness, sadness, perfectionism, inner criticism combined with self-criticism, and self-sabotage are just a few of the obstacles to overcome before the individual can make peace with her character.

Apart from these, the daughter may also live with the fear of becoming her mother and showing similar narcissistic traits, creating a continuous sense of fear and self-loathing. Some warning signs of narcissistic role model conditioning are manipulative behavior, showing off, and self-absorbed attention. But, although narcissism is a form of abuse that can be passed on, you are in control to stop the cycle. Your abuse was real, but once you open your eyes, you can also end the damaging patterns. Not only will you recover for your own sake but also for the sake of your children and significant others who engage intimately with you. Re-mothering thus means to first understand your narcissistic mother, then to stop trying to change her, and lastly to self-mother your brokenness into a comprehensive wholeness.

Becoming Your Mother

Can a narcissistic mother lead to the child becoming a narcissistic daughter? We have seen that researchers are not clear on what the root causes are but there is a possibility. Understanding narcissism and being aware of its inheritability are the first steps to re-mothering yourself. We are all human and we exhibit certain traits; we all make mistakes. In later sections of the book, we will look at the important concept of forgiveness and the narcissistic mother. In this chapter, I will focus on re-mothering the victim.

Identifying Narcissistic Manifestations as the Victimized Daughter

Some narcissistic traits may develop in the daughter and they are primarily based on a resistance to criticism, acts of disobedience, and feelings of resentfulness. The daughter raised by a narcissistic mother may:

- Constantly need approval from various people. She may always look for credit and acknowledgment and constantly seek admiration.

- Not take direction. This also manifests similarly in attention deficit hyperactivity disorder (ADHD).

- Not follow advice and receive advice poorly. Use

rudeness and cruelty to enforce her own opinions. Counter-attack others to divert attention away from the self.

- Exhibit envy of siblings and play the victim.

- Take sides with one parent against the other.

- Overuse social media, combined with an overrated performance on social media, and play the victim on social media.

- Feel demeaned from inferior job levels and show a lack of respect for managers or superiors.

- Focus on appearance and make comparisons with the narcissistic mother. Show an overemphasis on the value of beauty.

- Have an unrealistically perceived jealousy of the mother.

- Display a high interest in inheritance. She may also exhibit a Machiavellian attitude. Machiavellians are highly charming individuals with a profound lack of consciousness who display disagreeableness, manipulative behavior, compulsive lying, cynical attitudes, cunning devices, indifference to moral values, malevolence, craftiness, and deceitfulness. They are generally highly destructive and it's best to avoid contact with them. The term is based on the literary classic book by the Italian diplomat Niccolo Machiavelli called *The Prince,* where the protagonist follows a political path of achieving goals remorselessly and without any consideration for others. Machiavellian people are often attracted to wealth and power and they would manipulate and control anything to obtain these.

When any of these traits sound familiar to you, uphold them as red flags for inheritability. You do not have to become your mother—an understanding of narcissism and taking deliberate action are strong tools for recovery. Being aware that your responses may also be narcissistic at times, since your primary role model conditioned your behavior in childhood, will level your eyes in the right direction.

Re-Mothering the Daughter

Re-mothering the daughter happens across borders of psychological, physical, and spiritual interference. Your drive for healing should manage the conscious and unconscious sides of your being because both were damaged.

Shadow Work

Carl Jung defined our shadow side almost 100 years ago as the parts of our being that we refuse to acknowledge, accept, or identify with. We are often ashamed of our shadow side, or sometimes even unaware of this hidden and suppressed side of our characters. We feel guilty about it but it tends to show itself in narcissistic interactions despite our efforts to prevent it. This results in profound feelings of shame, antipathy, hostility and rage, inferiority, envy, and also anxiety. Because we were always told to suppress and not show these dark sides of our personality, we then struggle to deal with the reactions and their accompanying emotions. This cycle repeats itself many times in our lives as a result of being conditioned by narcissism. Once we become aware of our dark side and accept and admit that we have it, we learn to express the shadow side in a non-destructive and more positive way, resulting in a less frightening and less controlling situation that enhances our personal development.

Shadow work relies on the paired acceptance of the light and the dark side of our personalities. We are beings composed of polarities and we cannot understand one without the other. Light has no meaning without its relation to darkness. Denying the existence of one denies the existence of both. We can only become whole when we embrace the whole of our being, even the unwanted side. Victims of narcissistic abuse often have no boundaries between these polarities, leaving them confused and stuck. Recovering is a three-step process that begins with bringing the unconscious to the surface, identifying our automated responses (like running away from conflict or auto-responding to please everybody and avoid conflict as if all people are abusers), and lastly, getting more insight into being whole. Shadow work starts by aligning our behavior (including the conditioned ones) with our core beliefs in order to reprogram our character. Becoming whole involves a clearer understanding of our toxic shame, the guilt we feel, and the anger that hovers below the surface. It's a painful process to turn the inward shame toward the outside, to acknowledge, and face the shame—but with the correct guidance and patience, working on this part of our personality brings enormous soothing.

An example may be where you were ignored as a child when you asserted yourself. If your mother simply did not listen to you, you eventually resorted to a more aggressive communication style in order to be heard (shouting, crying, cursing, etc.). This validated your dysfunctional communication style, which easily gets triggered in adult life and in other circumstances. Feelings of guilt appear when the dark side shows and you become upset with yourself for losing grace. Taking these 'exiled' parts of ourselves into our hands and caring for them helps to re-mother what we lost. You learn to improve your relational interaction and, while becoming whole, you are discovering new, healthier ways to communicate and meet your needs that don't cause so much destruction.

Physical Recovery

Physical symptoms from emotional abuse have varying intensity and manifest differently depending on the time span of traumatic exposure. Many of them are muscle tension-related. You may develop unresolved aches and pains without any particular origin. Racing heartbeats, tremors, and tension headaches can all be symptomatic of an abusive childhood (unless they are related to substance use or medication). The child may develop concentration difficulties, digestive issues, or fibromyalgia. This is a disorder of musculoskeletal pain that relates to fatigue, mood, and memory issues. It is believed that fibromyalgia affects the way that the spinal cord and the brain process pain signals.

To help your physical recovery it is important to nurture a healthy empathy with yourself. Your narcissistic mother showed a complete lack of empathy as your primary caregiver. She did not nurture you like mothers are supposed to nurture. Re-mothering yourself implies nurturing your broken soul. Salvage the empathy you never received and focus the empathy on yourself, not only on others.

In some cases, the mother showered the daughter with financial benefits or excessive gifting. In other cases, she manipulated you by withholding financial support. It takes an effort to walk away from these constraints that have become a familiarity to you. It helps to understand that they are not normal and they are contributing to the dysfunctional relationship between you and your mother. To re-mother this child means to make peace and let go of the materialistic gains or losses.

Another constraint that has to be banished is the covert aggression (as well as the underlying passive aggression) from the narcissistic mother. The aggression may have included sexual molestation, humiliation, or allowing others to sexually abuse you while she was looking on. Acknowledgment and processing of these involve professional guidance and the severity and intensity of the damage should never be underestimated or overlooked. You have the right to respect. You have the right to trust. You have the right to say no to violations. You have the right to safety. Most importantly, you have the right to voice them.

Emotional Awareness

Making emotional improvements to your wholeness

involves managing perfectionism, understanding compulsive habits, and addressing unresolved fears. It also means enforcing your agreed boundaries as your defense against your narcissistic mother's gaslighting and silent treatment, her raging and interrogating abuse, her guilt-tripping, nit-picking, and invalidating of your truth. When you deliberately and mindfully apply these on a daily basis, you reshape your self-worth and rebuild your strength. Eventually, you allow yourself to become the person you were meant to be and not the projected image that your dysfunctional mother imposed on you.

The daughter of a narcissistic mother was exposed to continuous dichotomous thinking. Most narcissists function in a black and white world and they impose that on you so that they do not lose their defense mechanisms. They love to do splitting. Whether they are dividing siblings or whether they are dividing your thoughts for you, they cannot fathom gray areas and their thought processes are typically "either/or" operated. Your narcissistic mother may have conditioned and projected these binary thought processes onto you so it is important to remember not to make hasty decisions when you are also prone to dichotomous thought processes.

Spiritual Support

Spirituality does not necessarily imply a belief in a specific religion. For some individuals, a religious base may be beneficial on a healing road to re-mothering the self. Others may need more diversity. I prefer to define a spiritual approach as a healthy ritualistic devotion in order to improve the self and inflict less harm on others. The choice of your spiritual (or religious) journey will be different from another person's precisely because we are all unique individual beings with unique archetypal histories, and this is why we choose different options on our spiritual journeys. One person may find the devotion to a karate practice beneficial; another may find yoga stimulating, and another may find tranquility in meditation, chanting, confessing to a priest, or caring for houseplants and stray animals. The crucial concept is that the anchoring of spiritual devotion finds strength in your habits.

Maintaining a positive outlook (despite the challenging days when darkness overwhelms) is useful too for personal development. Of course, it is normal to have good and bad days when you are re-mothering your vulnerability, and I firmly believe that the bad days are just as useful when you are able to acknowledge and accept them for their positive purpose toward growth and understanding. The strength lies in the choice that you make to feel them, to be curious about them, to understand them, and then to separate them from your current reality. This in itself is a habitual spiritual devotion. It brings more self-awareness which improves self-trust, which improves trust in others, which creates better relationships, and which ultimately releases peace of mind inside a new wholeness.

Choosing Unconditional Love

Choosing to love and receive unconditional love without predetermined conditions, qualifications, and exceptions starts with loving yourself in the present moment. For some of us, love does not come easily and naturally, we have to work at it with a daily mindful approach. We have to deliberately choose to become more vulnerable, recognize the things that trigger our shadow sides, and nurture our self-worth. My personal struggle for love as the invisible child has been to find worth and to give myself the right to be someone. My sister's search for love (as the golden child) has been a constant struggle to outperform herself in every environment. We both ended up with a history of conflict, disappointment, and loneliness that permeated our work and relational environments. I finally understand after all these years that we were allowed to embrace a healthy self-concept. Our mother made us believe the opposite, though.

Self-Expression

Self-expression starts when you find your identity in the good and the bad, the light and the dark. It is easy to love ourselves when we achieve something but to love ourselves when we make mistakes requires a non-judgmental approach without pre-conditions to our self-love. This is the real test of recovery and re-mothering your broken self. To do this we have to separate our flawed actions from our character. We have to nurture our humanly flawed identity and stop demanding perfection from ourselves in every situation. Remember that self-esteem is how we 'feel' about ourselves, but acceptance is merely acknowledging who you have become, flaws and all. It's an affirmation of the self that lays the stepping stones for positive self-improvement. Accepting your reality may be difficult at times and you may not like your truth but by accepting yourself you regain balance. Balance fosters calm and confidence. Confidence harbors healthy and unconditional self-expression. The aim is to "be on your side when you implement change" and not to constantly say to yourself that you "do not like yourself."

Emotional Expression

After accepting ourselves we can focus on the emotional expression of relearning to feel. Learning to be vulnerable again may be frightening at first. As an abused child you were conditioned to hide your feelings as a defense mechanism. As an adult outside the dysfunctional environment, you have to listen to your body, allow yourself to speak, allow yourself to voice an opinion, and allow your fragile being to show emotion. You may feel irritable, numb, or even suffer from constant mood swings. Narcissistic abuse triggered an abandonment wound that requires healing. Feel these emotions freely without demands or restrictions and allow yourself expression, because only through releasing them do we find tranquility.

Liberating the Being

Only after acceptance do we improve ourselves in a meaningful way and are we able to come unstuck from a cycle of entrapment. It has been proved that unresolved traumatic experiences in our lives have a tendency to resurface, many times at the most vulnerable moments, only to cause profound distress and damage. We will discuss the effects of complex trauma in chapter 7 but it is important to note here that liberation of our damaged selves depends on releasing the past and separating it from the present. And it implies facing the dysfunctions, conditioning, and trauma—not merely letting it go by ignoring it. Facing our demons enables us to be free of them.

Banishing the Narcissistic Cycle

I have discussed the importance of boundaries and disengagement. Sometimes these boundaries imply termination and ceasing contact with your narcissistic mother. In extreme cases, this may be the only way to take back your power. It may be challenging to implement the separation so harshly, but in other situations, it may bring instant relief. However, the separation takes place, it is important to know that you have to banish the cycle with deliberate effort and maintain the change.

Gratitude Practices

Gratitude is a proactive coping strategy that has proved itself to be useful in recovery from narcissistic trauma. Methods to encourage gratitude can be gift-giving, meditation, charity work, writing a letter to someone, or simply sending someone a social media notification like a compliment. You will be delightfully surprised at the feedback! I suggest a gratitude journaling method. If you can make the time daily to find a meaningful anchor to hold you while you are removing yourself from a narcissistic environment, then you have already run half of the race. There may be days when these anchors are very hard to see and ever more challenging to find. On those days, I have simply told myself many times that I value my cat's presence. Just that simple awareness of not being alone has helped me through the mire of the day until my strength was better. And writing it down somewhere can be a reminder of gratitude on those days when you are completely unable to find something. It simply involves finding something that is valuable to us.

If you do not believe me, here are some real-life examples that researchers have found:

> Veterans with higher levels of gratitude after serving in the Vietnam War were found to have lower PTSD rates, for one, and a study of 9-11 survivors revealed that it helped to improve resilience (Fredrickson et al., 2003; Kashdan et al., 2006). In Indonesian earthquake victims, it was discovered that gratitude had a positive impact on their health and PTSD symptoms, suggesting it aids our recovery from traumatic experiences (Lies et al., 2014). And in Israeli teenagers who had lived through heavy missile attacks, it played a pivotal role in helping them reframe their difficult contexts, viewing their situations in a positive way despite the odds (Israel-Cohen et al., 2014), (Moore, 2019).

Gratitude practices do not deliver immediate results, and just like all the other recovery practices after childhood trauma, success and efficiency depend on our devotion to mindfully apply them all on a daily basis. The concept of gratitude revolves around the fact that we adapt our perception of fear-inducing stress as a mere challenge, instead of perceiving it as a threat. Now I can work with that...

Returning to the Feminine

We all have masculine and feminine energy that is regulated by the left and the right side of the brain regardless of our gender. Masculine energy focuses on the more rational aspects and on receiving an end result, while feminine energy is the more creative and imaginative energy. It is sometimes called the left and right brain functioning. The important thing is to have these two energies in balance in order to function harmoniously. The narcissist operates with unbalanced energies, and your exposure to a narcissistic mother may result in overexposure to masculine energy at times. You then compensate with an over-presentation of feminine energy, resulting in an underdeveloped ego and reduced confidence blocking you from getting things done.

Another gender aspect that may impact narcissistic victims is societal stereotypes. Many times, female victims of abuse are further traumatized by stereotypical beliefs of societies that tend to blame victims instead of the abusers. Combined with the possibility of manipulative narcissistic charm that the abuser uses to defend him/herself, these stereotypes enable the false narrative that the female victim internalizes and starts believing.

She ends up believing that she is the problem and also has to cope with the suffering of abusive trauma. As a result, many female victims end up believing that they are unlovable, unworthy of love, and ugly, while more depression, frustration, and alienation set in.

To change this, it is useful to first understand this societal and environmental imbalance. Then the individual should separate that from their character. Women are innately nurturing beings. We give and we would like to receive care and love. Taking small steps toward self-nurturing and gaining clearer awareness of narcissistic dysfunction, combined with meditation and healthy moments in natural environments, is a crucial process to return to your feminine strength and reclaim your power as an individual.

Takeaway Guidelines

- Personalities can be molded; you have the power to reinvent yourself.

- You have a clear guideline of narcissistic manifestations that you can flag if they appear externally or internally.

- Your refusal to become your mother starts by looking at your shadow side, listening to your body's warning signs, analyzing your emotions with a keen curiosity, and taking the lead from spiritual devotion.

Calls to Action

- Your mother failed you in motherhood; grieve the loss, and do not allow this to fail yourself by not letting her go.

- Express your identity and your emotions in order to liberate yourself.

- Banish the devastating narcissistic cycle by returning to your vulnerable feminine side and reinventing your power with practicing gratitude.

Chapter 7

CPTSD Recovery

That's why I want to address CPTSD here and to encourage those who feel overwhelmed or hopeless to realize they are not broken. They are injured, and these injuries are treatable.
–Robyn Brickel

Trauma is a risk factor for many personality disorders. The effects of trauma can feature in disorders like borderline personality disorder (BPD), substance use disorder (SUD), various anxiety disorders, and so forth. The symptoms of trauma also surface in a variety of ways.

Most people are aware of post-traumatic stress disorder (PTSD) but few people differentiate between this and complex post-traumatic stress disorder (CPTSD). According to the Mayo Clinic, PTSD is a health condition that is preceded by a traumatic event that causes severe anxiety, flashbacks, nightmares, and uncontrollable thoughts about the specific triggering event (Mayo Clinic Staff, 2018). For a diagnosis to be made of CPTSD, the individual has to show criteria of PTSD, but very importantly and in addition to these, the individual must also display secondary symptoms. This is the differentiating factor for CPTSD diagnosis. These additional symptoms focus on disturbances and self-organization, specifically affective factors like emotion dysregulation, a negative self-concept, and interpersonal issues.

Research has found that families who appear externally like "high achieving families" who also manifest "emotional neglect" are just as damaging as "active violence in deprived families" (The School of Life, 2020). An excellent example of a CPTSD diagnosis can be after a caregiver betrays a victim, resulting in a long-term traumatic experience.

What is CPTSD?

If you relate to feeling trapped, either from clamping or from trudging or feeling abandoned, and you are craving an escape—address your complex trauma. PTSD is classically defined in the International Classification of Diseases (ICD-11) with symptoms of intrusions, hyperreactivity, and avoidance. CPTSD is further defined as a subtype or subgroup of PTSD, resulting from various types of long-term trauma, and from which escape was either too dangerous or impossible. The inescapability factor makes the diagnosis different. The emotional dysregulation, attachment and interpersonal relationship difficulties, and reactivity to relationships resulting from this are generally based on fear and anger later in life. A predominantly negative shift in self-perception is prominent. The individual perceives herself as damaged, shamed, easily blames herself, believes herself to be deserving of maltreatment, and has a distorted image of the perpetrator in dysfunctional relationships. Apart from being mainly fear-based, it also shows more dissociative and avoidant tendencies, attention difficulties, anxiety arousal, difficulties with social engagement, exaggerated response, and hypervigilance than PTSD. The most prominent symptoms of a person suffering from CPTSD are as follows:

- They are hypervigilant and perceive the world as hostile and unsafe.

- They appear rigid and never relax, while having trouble with being touched. The anxiety may cause physical issues like bowel complications.

- They are easily alarmed and suffer from sleep disruptions.

- An appalling self-image haunts them. They feel like a burden and this concept is based on their perception of shame and being shamed.

- They are drawn to unavailable people because this allows them a safe and distant interactive space.

- Clinginess in other people is perceived as threatening and avoided at all costs. Ironically, they do crave to be loved.

- They lose their temper easily (with themselves and others) and may often look malicious and unfriendly, but they are actually scared and defenseless.

- Being alone is attractive and it presents blissful isolation for them.

- They feel paranoid and constantly suspect hostility from others. The social media arena is an especially hostile environment for them. Their deep sense of mistrust starts with the self and also involves others.

- They can throw themselves into work and focus obsessively on their careers while finding holidays or retirement difficult.

- They experience living as an exhausting and unpleasant endeavor and idealize not having to live.

- They are often rigid about routines, show no spontaneity, clean often, and are generally perceived by others as being overly 'OCD.'

Some overlapping symptoms of comorbidities make the diagnosis of CPTSD difficult. An understanding of the similarities and differences helps to direct treatment, once the diagnosis has been defined. CPTSD often gets confused with BPD. The overlapping features show the following key differences between BPD and CPTSD.

BPD is a mental health disorder categorized in the DSM. It has the highest suicidal rate and self-harming features, it exhibits an unstable identity, and a definite love-hate cycle of the self. Sometimes an individual with BPD may not have a significant traumatic past experience, but CPTSD always has at least one period of an inescapable, long-term, traumatic past experience. Many similar symptoms do not always manifest to the same degree as with CPTSD. The key differentiating symptoms of BPD are high levels of self-harm and suicidal components, intense avoidance and fear of abandonment, paranoia, impulsivity, and an exaggerated unstable sense of the self (it can be a negative perception the one day and a positive one the next day).

CPTSD is not a DSM categorized disorder (it is defined in the ICD-11) and does not have a strong suicidal variant. Suicidal ideation issues are normally based on an escape from the perceived unpleasantness of the world, rather than a desire for death. The individual presents a distorted identity with a more persistently negative and damaged self-perception that remains fairly stable. It differs from BPD which associates with the "I don't know who I am" view of the self. Distrust combined with 'numbing' and feeling distant in relationships take place. Negative self-talk causes many negative mood symptoms that prevail. Anger outbursts happen in CPTSD, relationships are not perceived as safe spaces, and the individual devalues themself. Chronic abandonment struggles are not typical in CPTSD, individuals experience more of a fear of the relationship itself.

Another major difference between the two is noticeable in the materialization of relationship separation and relationship difficulties. In BPD the individual fluctuates between devaluation and idealization of the partner, combined with initiating new relationships rapidly. CPTSD individuals tend to end or avoid relationships in times of extreme stress. CPTSD is nearly always based on complex trauma which started in childhood. These events could be sexual abuse, emotional neglect, bullying, humiliation, violence, anger, or disrupted attachment which increased a sense of guilt, mood dysregulation, and a negative self-concept.

Recovery—A Long Term Healing Journey

Recovery means you are a survivor! Even though this idea may feel disturbing, it is worthwhile knowing that survival comes with solutions. The feelings of insecurity, being unsafe, and feeling overwhelmed are simply your body's normal response to your trauma. Therefore, a therapeutic, progressively phased approach that focuses on safety and security, memory and grief, and reconnecting the self remains the basis for a successful healing journey. You want to feel in control and more comfortable in your body instead of constantly hovering (or trudging) in a triggered state of alarm. The healing starts by noticing the impact of the trauma, and through an awareness of the difference between the past 'truth' and the current 'reality.' Let us focus on a few methods to regain your sense of self.

Developing Calm and Tranquility

A person who suffers from PTSD has nightmares, flashbacks, and constant anxiety. The same happens with CPTSD. The body is conditioned to respond to an overactive fight-or-flight-or-freeze habit. Relationships are definite triggers for dysfunctional responses and therefore, creating safety and security is a key undertaking in the recovery process. The first step is to create a sense of calmness and stability that will enhance a feeling of emotional and physical safety.

Therapy assists with acquiring appropriate skills to teach your body how to feel and how to recognize a safe environment. The specific skills may vary, depending on the traumatic scenarios, as well as the individual's personality. (Skill examples may be engaging in outdoor activities, relaxation techniques like breathing and meditation, confiding in a trusted person, joining a support group, or even spending time alone in nature.) These are extremely important and they will give your body the support it needs. You will learn that you will not always be punished or hurt when you express your needs, thoughts, and feelings.

Physical, psychological, and emotional support are vital for healthy human interaction. Once you feel protected, you can focus on the succeeding steps and when life becomes overwhelming again, come back to this basic first step to find your calmness again. In tranquility lies your power of recovery that was taken from you during childhood.

Remembrance and Mourning

The body remembers. It often happens that the trauma survivor is unable to identify or name the specific trauma, she simply feels a sensation that is triggered by a bodily response after exposure to a memory. She experiences a threatening moment and finds a way to cope with the feelings. The same coping mechanisms are conditioned over the years to block the feelings. Becoming present in your body helps to create manageable feelings without being overwhelmed into a fight-or-flight-or-freeze response while the trauma is being processed.

Remembering and mourning the loss is the second and most vital step en route to recovery. This is often the most difficult part and many people avoid this phase only to end up never recovering from the trauma. Reprocessing the trauma and the reconsolidation of old memories are crucial to recovery. Avoiding this may simply create alternative coping mechanisms. It is important to be actively engaged in this phase and the guidance of supportive and gentle therapy will create a containing environment for this challenging process. You are basically mourning the loss of the things you never had, comparable to the loss of a loved one. Stop trying to change your mother in a futile attempt to win her approval. It is almost impossible and you simply exhaust yourself and decrease your sense of self-worth. Moving forward means letting the mother go.

There are various therapy options available that assist efficiently with this phase e.g., eye movement desensitization and reprocessing (EMDR), cognitive behavioral therapy (CBT), neurofeedback therapy, or trauma processing therapy. Trauma-based therapy appears to be the most effective since it focuses on both sensations and cognitive processes. It has a higher success rate as the client focuses on distancing the present from the past. When the traumatized client can put the danger separately in the past, the individual is able to move forward with a dual awareness into a safer and more peaceful present.

Reconnection and Integration

"Your behavior makes sense, given what has happened to you" (Brickel et al., 2019). It is important to understand that you were exposed to trauma that made you feel powerless. Many survivors of CPTSD believe that their traumatic experiences were normal, or "not that bad", or even worse, that the trauma was their own fault. This is a false perception of reality and enables your ignorance of something that should take priority. The only way to heal is to acknowledge that you were only a helpless child and had no power to change the circumstances. It is important to understand that the trauma was indeed bad and certainly not normal. Redefining a sense of safety and security, something that was very unfamiliar because you had no reference point for what reality could be like, is a crucial step in the recovery process.

You have to remember that the "trauma parts" are no longer current, nor do they exist in the present. Nurture the "protective parts" of the self that developed in the trauma survivor. Trauma-informed caring of the present self is based on a memory of how you survived from what 'happened' to you, instead of focusing on the false truths that your conditioning forced on your self-image. This approach immediately puts the event outside of your body. Using a strength-based trauma-informed healing model makes the individual aware that the fault is not with them per se; it accepts the person for who they are. "You heal by being present in yourself" (Brickel, 2021). Rediscovering yourself is liberating.

Emotional scars may take years to recover. Because CPTSD enables fragmentation (when the brain removes parts of the memory to help the individual cope with reality) and dissociation (the experience of never feeling present), you turn toward coping methods (for example drugs, alcohol, sex, food, etc.) to block the pain. Healthy reconnection, resolution, and reconsolidation of past events combined with a healthy integration in the present taking place with professional guidance help the cognitive and emotive processes to redefine themselves inside a safe space. In this phase, you are able to establish safety as well as engage with mourning the loss in order to experience tranquility, without the trauma hanging over your head like a dark and threatening cloud. Here we find a new voice instead of feeling constantly victimized and harassed by the past. It is also in this phase that helping others can give purpose to our own past suffering, and thus liberate us from dwelling in the past.

Seeking Therapy

Some classical therapeutic interventions (like CBT) aim to change the cognitive processes of how we perceive and understand triggers and our emotive responses to them. This approach may have limitations when it comes to trauma-based issues because the focus is on changing the thought processes instead of the actual events. It makes more sense for CPTSD to have a trauma-based therapeutic focus that specifically confronts and deals with the trauma. When focusing on dysregulated stress responses, feelings, and listening to the bodily sensations, priority is given to guiding the individual to face and recognize the trauma. In this way, creating healthy life-saving stress responses opens the gateway to healing.

Efficient healing is furthermore based on a therapeutic relationship where the client and the psychologist/psychiatrist create a safe space together where trauma and triggers can be identified, acknowledged, and addressed without feeling overwhelmed. With the guidance of professional help, the client looks at the reasons for the feelings and triggers in a contained environment. The therapist-client relationship is crucial to enabling the client's own relationship improvement as the healing journey progresses. Integration in this way assists with the development of more healthy regulation of emotions and feelings.

> Trauma-informed therapy with a bottom-up approach allows a person to explore the dysregulated feelings *after* safety and stabilization are built and felt. Safety and stability allow a person to have one foot in feelings (right side of the brain or bottom) and one foot in the logic, the here and now, the present, the frontal lobe (left side or top) (Brickel et al., 2019).

A treatment plan should be designed individually for clients based on the occurrence of specific symptoms and the client's environment or circumstances. Clients who are diagnosed with both CPTSD and BPD should receive a different approach to recovery than an individual who only manifests CPTSD. In both instances the emphasis should be on decreasing dependence, improving a positive self-concept, and managing suicidal tendencies or ideation. Successful treatment also depends on incorporating methods of decreasing social avoidance, empowerment of the self, and compassion toward the younger self. An efficient therapist walks with you to a place of safety where you experience less fear and less shame and fosters a reviewed sense of purpose to move forward. With a professional person holding your hand step by step, you are taking back your life.

Managing Well-Being

Someone made us feel unsafe and judged in the past for an extended period. Someone also failed to provide a kind and stable environment that encouraged healthy development and acceptance. The root cause of CPTSD was an absence of love and therefore the primary treatment should prioritize the relearning of loving the self again (whom the individual has come to hate so much). This is an ongoing and mindful daily process in maintaining well-being that requires commitment from the victimized survivor. Just like we focus on exercise to keep the body healthy, the concept of keeping the brain 'fit' with devoted practice may help to manage well-being. Different parts of the brain help us to understand and use information while also teaching us how to survive. Polyvagal exercises and neuroplasticity are two modalities of neurological exercise that assist well-being.

The concept of neuroplasticity focuses on habit-forming actions of doing the same practices continuously over a period of time, to reshape the brain with a positive outcome. Neuroplasticity is a disciplined and mindful recreation of yourself. "What you pay attention to, what you think and feel and want, and how you react and behave all physically shape your brain" (Hampton, 2014). This can be practiced in conjunction with formal therapy.

Dr. Stephen Porges explains the concept of polyvagal theory as a "neuroplatform for expression." The theory explains the connection of the nervous system to our responses, the nervous system processes based on past experiences, and how it monitors and regulates the functioning of our organs, either to mobilize or relax the body. The three states that are created (a state of safety, a state of fight-flight, or a state of freeze) help us to navigate and cope in situations. Past trauma, for example from child abuse, creates more state of freeze symptoms like anxiety, depression, isolation, etc. Other traumatic experiences instigate other responses.

Problems arise when an individual misinterprets human expression on an inter-relational basis. A traumatized individual may interpret and perceive neutral faces as aggressive, or a fearful face as angry. A person with a history of abuse or socializing dysfunction (resulting from abusive parenting styles) is not always able to use and interpret body language from other people to self-regulate, and inter-relational issues develop.

Strategies to retrain automatic responses involve adjustment of breathing, focus on sensory information, identification and mindfulness of misinterpretation, and adjustment of posture and movements. Because information is generally evaluated on a subconscious level, it is helpful to read the physical signs of the body. A pounding heart, back pain, or a headache may all be providing bodily information about the neural circuits that support your behavior.

In my experience, the road to recovery is made up of a combination of actions, deliberate psychological and dietary changes, therapeutic support, corporeal awareness, and meaningful interactions. Every minute of every day shapes our brain as it shapes our being. There may have been a time when we did not understand this and when the significant others who were supposed to guide us failed us. But we have survived with a magnitude of resilience and knowledge that we can apply with a selfless commitment to ourselves. We deserve to live and we can finally say it without fear or shame!

Takeaway Guidelines

- BPD, PTSD, and CPTSD all point to a prominent defining aspect of abusive victimization, namely trauma. It is crucial to identify and process the traumatic experiences in order to recover.

- Complex trauma is associated with narcissistic abuse and it is based on the inescapability from repetitive traumatic events.

- Therapeutic intervention takes many forms and depends on each individual scenario and history.

- The most efficient way to reconnect and manage your well-being is through focusing on remembering and mourning, integrating, developing tranquility, and putting the traumatic events outside your body by deliberate separation.

Calls to Action

- Recovery means you have survived!

- Trauma recovery depends on separation, step-by-step recovery in a contained environment, identifying and maintaining your physical and mental well-being, and gently rebuilding yourself with the guidance of a professional therapist.

- You have the right to live after pain!

CHAPTER 8

Liberation & Healing Guidelines

There is no growth without real feeling. Children not loved for who they are do not learn how to love themselves. Their growth is an exercise in pleasing others, not in expanding through experience. As adults, they must learn to nurture their own lost child.
–Marion Woodman

Forgiveness is a crucial element in recovering from the rage and frustration that linger in the abused child. The sad reality is that it is impossible to fix the broken relationship with your mother. You ended up with copious amounts of internalized anger because your needs were not met. Forgiveness implies the acceptance of people for who they are. When you are willing to become curious about them instead of focusing on your personal loss, you take responsibility for your own needs and the healing happens. In this chapter, we will focus on this significant healing journey.

The psychological benefits of forgiveness are associated with decreased mental and physical health problems, like increased hopefulness and a healthier sense of the self. It also lowers anxiety levels, reduces anger, and facilitates less depression. Even when reconciliation is not a possibility, forgiving still brings relief—this point helps to understand the concept of forgiveness. Forgiveness is actually very similar to rejection but the main difference is that rejection has no positive emotions directed at the offender because it's more pragmatic. So, if you consider the relationship with your narcissistic mother in the same category as, for example, a job offer rejection, the distancing facilitates the process of forgiveness. The main difference is that in a primary relationship, the memories still remain despite the failure to invest in a connection.

It is also beneficial to understand that hatred cannot foster forgiveness, but rejection can. So, in order to forgive, it is crucial to address the rage and the hatred before you reject (or more softly said: separate) the narcissistic abuse or the person per se. By forgiving, you are eliminating negative thoughts about the offender and developing positive thoughts. Forgiving and forgetting are necessary simultaneously in order to move on and to heal, not only from our mother but also in our other relationships with partners, friends, colleagues, and children. Simply forgetting does not solve the trauma and neither does forgiving when you still hold the memory close.

Remember that you were part of a one-sided relationship where one person only cared about herself and the other cared about both. This understanding of the abuser encourages the process of forgiveness. The following basic steps toward forgiveness give structure to a very challenging process.

- Lamenting the wrongdoing and familiarizing yourself with your own needs.

- Finding the grudge within yourself, establishing empathy toward the offender, and considering if you are willing to let it go.

- Identifying one similarity and one difference between your mother and yourself. This makes you realize that you have a right to be, just like she has the right to be (distorted or dysfunctional as it seems).

- Developing a lifestyle of forgiveness. This involves forgiving yourself as well. You have to forgive yourself for staying in the relationship and even for abandoning the relationship.

Reframing your concept of who you are and where you are in relation to others brings healing. Your mother chose to stay the way she is, you cannot change her, when you accept this, you are able to move on. You only have the power to change yourself. Let her linger in her own confusion and remove yourself from it. By putting your needs first again and prioritizing yourself without guilt feelings, you are able to liberate your being.

> Healing from a narcissistic parent has a positive effect on all of the other close relationships in a [person's] life. The distorted perception of reality a narcissistic parent imposes on a child can have damaging consequences as an adult at work and home. The lack of self-esteem, obsessive thinking, minimization of abuse, excessive anxiety, and fear-based reactions are common among adult children of narcissists. By addressing the impact of narcissism, a person finds relief (Hammond, 2016).

The Healing Journey of the Daughter

What happens to the daughter who fails to meet her narcissistic mother's perception? She is bombarded with emotional punishment which includes manipulation, invalidation, withholding affection, withdrawal, and neglect. The most prominent image I still have of my 'childhood' mother is the woman sitting in the dark living room with swollen red eyes from all her crying after she had an argument with my father. The latter always ended up outside in his shed or the garden after these arguments, where he could hide his pain while whistling to recover his trapped breathing. Of course, they were both at fault during these argumentative periods, it takes two to tango (such a terrible cliché but still the most powerful way of describing the dance between two intimate souls) but until this day I vividly remember the heaviness surrounding my mother against the aching surrounding my father. It was almost as if she wanted everybody to know that she was suffering the most intensely. As the child in the background of these outbursts, I became acutely aware of being in the way while feeling compelled to restore the tranquility to the scene and to both of them. But I also became intensely aware that I would always fail at restoring harmony with her because she would turn any gesture into an attack or intrusion. I learned to hide my feelings and I became invisible in an attempt to avoid punishment for something that I didn't even do. I started to fear retribution.

The healing journey of the daughter who suffered prolonged emotional trauma is guided by a few crucial actions.

- Identify places and moments of experiencing overreactions in your current environment. Look for physical clues in your body (like a racing heart, a warm feeling on your forehead, etc.). Unresolved trauma is generally triggered like this. Follow the sensations, identify the images that come to mind, experience the feelings, and analyze the resulting thoughts to discover the gaps in your narrative of past trauma.

- Write down ten traumatic experiences that you recall. They may vary in intensity but the idea is to force your mind to think of at least ten incidents. (Some people may come up with many more.) Because our brain tends to forget traumatic experiences, in this way we force ourselves to bring to light the events that affected us, and some that we have forgotten or buried.

- Think through the distorted timeline and gaps in the narrative. Reflect and make the narrative coherent.

- Use the RAIN approach to calm down any distress that may arise from these memories. The RAIN approach is recommended by psychologists Tara Brach and Jack Kornfield and the acronym stands for "recognizing the loss/pain/trauma and resulting feeling, acknowledging the resulting present emotion, investigating the relation of the present feeling to your past experience, and non-identification of the experience where you do not allow the moment to define you but instead remind yourself that it is merely a memory."

- Gather additional information from trusted significant others when there are gaps in your memory. This will clarify your perspective. What matters most is the meaning of the experience, not so much the experience itself.

- Do not rationalize the overwhelming feelings but accept them for what they are without judgment. Feeling the full impact of the pain is an important step to processing and resolving the trauma and thus recovering some relief from the event.

- Write them down patiently without judgment and with self-compassion.

- Tell your story to a trusted person who can provide valuable and honest insight and perspective.

To liberate yourself from the toxic past, focus on improving the following concepts in your life. Keep the recovery focus primarily directed at yourself. Now that you have taken all the steps to protect yourself from your narcissistic mother (boundaries, disengagement, separation, etc.) the time has come to nurture yourself. Make a daily habit of this and stay mindful of your healing progress.

Releasing of Overwhelming Emotions

To manage frustrations and maternal provoking (where the mother plays the victim in response to your behavior) you will have to maintain and enforce your newly set boundaries. There is no benefit in reliving the traumatic experiences over and over again. Neither do you have to expose yourself to the same triggers ad finitum.

Unresolved trauma can make us suffer indefinitely. Research has proved that regardless of the intensity or the occurrence of traumatic events, the defining factor for recovery is processing these traumatic events. If they are left unresolved, we remain stuck in our pain. In addition to this, it is recommended to process trauma immediately after it occurred or as soon as possible after the event. Failing to do so may result in memory loss and alterations that can impact the coherent narrative toward recovery. Memory flashbacks, memory gaps, and alterations in memory are all normal consequences of surviving trauma. Be patient with yourself and use them to reach a more fulfilled understanding of the narcissistic patterns and manifestations.

Processing the events that took place in our childhood years in a coherent way will make us feel less fragmented. It may relieve accompanying shaming emotions when we realize that we were not responsible for certain events that happened beyond our control but still impact our being in a profound way. When we process the events individually in this way, we garner compassion and kindness toward ourselves. In this way, we gradually liberate ourselves from the grip of narcissistic manipulation and abuse.

You are also allowed to speak up. Particularly the invisible child and the scapegoat child may suffer from an enforced inability and innate fear to express themselves. It's safe to speak and it is safe to keep quiet when speaking does not contribute to any positive outcome. The power of speech and listening remains in your hands.

Emotional Intelligence

Regaining an emotional intelligence and maturity that functions in wholeness are a challenge. There are so many aspects of fragmentation to integrate into some coherent and functional concept that the mere attempt causes overwhelming emotions in itself. But then, every success story starts with one step, that difficult first step… Trust your intuition. I would say that the core issues to address are the following.

- Abandonment and rejection—even the golden child suffers some form of abandonment at the hand of the narcissistic mother. Your aim should be to work back toward an integrated being (away from the fragmentation) of your adult self. Your growth and maturity are made up of the parts of the younger you that cannot be denied. When you separate them from your narcissistic mother's abuse by applying a healthy curiosity to the development and manifestation of the different parts as you analyze them, they become the integrated wholeness of your individuality. Harness that.

- Hypervigilance—there is a reason why your body screams symptoms. Make them work for you and use them as a guide to information. Be curious about their existence and the root of their cause.

- Detachment—whether you choose detachment or whether it happens naturally as a result of narcissistic abuse, stay with the separation. Make the most of the option. The cliché expression "silence is golden" is indeed very calming. From a narcissistic victim's point of view, we can add gentleness to the silence equation as opposed to a manipulatively enforced silence.

- Stop continually questioning yourself and your sense of awareness, stop doubting your perceptions, stop hearing your mother's invalidating voice, and instead start listening to your inner strength.

- Gain a healthy perspective of realities. Your narcissistic mother had a distorted view of reality that she imposed on you that does not shape the current truth of your life. Step back, and counteract with a newly gained perspective. This will liberate you from false beliefs, lies, and mindless conditioning.

- Most of all, take this regained emotional stability into new relationships and find tranquility.

Releasing Blame and Shame

Release yourself from the toxic shame of narcissism. Narcissistic mothers have to feel superior and therefore constantly blame their daughters to establish compliance, obedience, and control. The blame takes place in various ways and often at the most inopportune times. Sometimes they may even turn a blind eye to their daughter being abused by someone else. They expose private information, they exaggerate your mistakes, or they even ignore/deny the shaming that happens to you as a result of their dysfunctional behaviors. They talk down to you or talk over you as if you do not exist, invalidating your right to be. They belittle you, compete with your achievements, and downplay your achievements. The list of blaming and shaming is endless. Fight this by being present. Deliberately separate abusive past experiences from your current life experiences of non-abusive events.

Understand, identify, and manage her gaslighting by ignoring or changing the topic. Believe in your perception and your worth. Remember you are not her projection; you are a strong survivor. Give up the quest of proving your narcissistic mother wrong. Her blaming you without reason was not your fault, it was a result of her own fears. Your constant effort to do more and achieve more (as a coping style) to win her validation eventually made you feel unfulfilled and disappointed. We always think that if we prove our mothers wrong they will see our worth, but we remain disillusioned when they don't. This feeling of being insignificant remains an overpowering emotion but the power is in your hands to release this cycle and avoid the negative patterns.

Implementing Non-Negotiable Boundaries

We have looked at the powerful effect of having boundaries that you implemented to protect yourself against your narcissistic mother. To retain your liberation and recovery it is crucial to stay mindful and committed to maintaining these non-negotiable boundaries. Manage what your mother perceives as "offensive attacks" and stay mindful of her manipulative tendencies and emotional hypervigilance. Maintaining the separation between your healthy perception and her distorted view of the world will enhance your confidence and give you the support to withstand any attacks from her. When you understand manipulation, you are able to identify and withstand it.

Self-Soothing

To counter your emotional numbing (the feeling of 'trudging' through life in a foggy state) it is important to remember that you do not have to be a perfect image to the world to be human or to be loved and respected or acknowledged. Guard against becoming the projection that your dysfunctional childhood system of narcissistic abuse enforced on you. Stop leading the life of the performer and start living. Soothe your worth by avoiding the negative internal criticism that keeps dragging you downwards on a self-harming spiral. Silence the chatter in your head that keeps invalidating you. You are not the helpless victim! Stop shrinking into a state of shame.

Depression and Anxiety

Mood disorders are a classic result of narcissistic abuse that impact our lives widely. Liberation and healing from them start with identifying the triggers that stimulate our conditioned trauma symptoms and behaviors. Most individuals will experience the triggers as a physical manifestation or an emotional reactivity. In extreme scenarios, our heightened startle reactions may present panic attacks or, for some individuals, manifestations of compulsive behavior. It is important to manage compulsive behavior that manifests in the work environment (e.g., becoming a workaholic), excessive hygienic fears, and cleanliness routines. I have found that "calling myself out" the moment when I realize that I am showing compulsive tendencies helps. It becomes a good practice to stop the behavior and reflect on the origin (the cause or reason) for the behavior, which is often stress or anxiety-related. Addressing the stressor instead of the compulsive behavior brings understanding and relief. With panic attacks, removing yourself from the scene and finding tranquility elsewhere (preferably in a natural environment) coupled with corrective breathing exercises is an effective regulator for combatting anxiety. Depression and overwhelming feelings of sadness and hopelessness require professional guidance. I believe that nobody should underestimate the power of these feelings. The miserable emotions that accompany them (like feeling isolated) can become life-threatening and should urgently be addressed.

Seeking Help and Speaking Up

Emotional abuse does not leave visible scars, making it more challenging to ask for help. Being conditioned to avoid healthy socializing during a narcissistic childhood compounds the effort to speak up and find professional help. It is therefore important to identify all the abusive behaviors first. Some may not be a priority but most abusive conditioning requires therapeutic intervention depending on the severity and the frequency.

By using the vast availability of various healing modalities (like neuroplasticity, CBT, polyvagal exercises, shadow work, EMDR, neurofeedback therapy, etc.) you will have the necessary support to create a foundation for safety and trust. Regaining a healthy perspective of safety will contribute to assisting your corrective relationship forming. Stability with relationships will enhance your self-esteem and confidence levels which eventually contribute to the general well-being in all other departments of your life.

Grieving the Mother

Grieving is a five-stage process that starts with denial, moves into anger, then bargaining, depression, and lastly, acceptance. But because a narcissistic childhood already forced you into constant bargaining and denial stages, you become stuck in sadness if you do not follow through to the acceptance stage. Accepting your loss(es) assists your internal processing of the feelings of sadness and anger into a healthier reality. The recovery happens once you realize that with narcissistic grieving, the worst is now in the past.

Grief is a natural and acceptable response to loss. It can happen because of divorce, a job loss, death, moving from a familiar home, or even a major transition or career change. Through grieving, we process the system of managing loss and with a natural bereavement period, sadness is a necessary result. However, narcissistic grief does not give the natural sadness of the bereavement phase because you are grieving many things at the same time. Your grief involves what would and could have been, a childhood, the loss of trust and faith in humanity, lost opportunities, the distortions of your concept of love and life, fairness and a just world, and so forth. A narcissistic childhood came with chronically experiencing disappointment that enhanced an undeniable melancholic heaviness that followed you into adulthood.

In your adult life, you may even experience the maintenance of relationships as a trigger for feelings of loss. Grief consequently repeats itself over and over again in other relationships. Some daughters experience grieving the pseudo-reality they made up during their lifetime to help cope with life. This creates many different negative mood states and the confusion comes with the yearning phase during loss. It is important to know that the yearning is in fact connected to fantasies you constructed about the relationship or to the bond with the trauma that creates an addictive compulsion to stay or get back into the narcissistic cycle. This is unhealthy grief. These are not realities and you are not grieving the person, you are grieving the loss of hope.

A profound feeling that may appear during a narcissistic loss is a longing for the beginning of the relationship or being the center of the narcissist's world. Children keep on wishing for a healthy parent and the need to hold on to that wish remains strong into adulthood. Attachment had to be maintained during the abuse; when this disappears, feelings of discomfort appear. Accepting the fact that you will never get what you wanted and making peace with the loss shifts the constant yearning over time even though the reality may initially feel viscerally inadequate.

Living the lie of not existing is a miserable position for any individual. Being the victim of numbing emotional abuse from constant narcissistic projection is exhausting and robs you of life. To recover from this, the victim has to deliberately 'dis-abuse' herself from the projection and damage, sit with it so that the projecting loses power, and then allow separation to take its course in order to eventually emerge as a more truthful and stronger self.

A scapegoat daughter grows up thinking that she is not good at all; the narcissistic mother forbids her to discover her true value and abilities because this would threaten the mother's authority, who tries to claim all achievements for herself. The vulnerable child starts to believe the mother because showing her talents would simply ensue an attack of jealousy, violation of her rights, or her successes being ripped away. She ends up being conditioned to manage her losses and diminish her self-worth. For the victimized child, this is much less traumatic than having to face the wrath of the mother and having to face a continuous sense of feeling inferior.

The ultimate challenge happens when this child's eyes open up and she has to confront the loss of a lifetime of self-worth that her mother banished from her. Like the invisible child, she has to cope with belittling, endless unrealistic comparisons, neglect, and abandonment when she matures. The favored daughter (the golden child) has to face other maternal losses. She has been conditioned throughout her life that she is special while receiving constant praises from the narcissistic mother. Unlike the invisible and scapegoat child, she did not have to compete for attention and acknowledgment. When the mother dies or when the golden child has to make a choice of separation from the enabling mother, she experiences profound confusion. She has been handicapped by the distortions of her mother and may find it challenging to suddenly earn her survival skills and achievements. Grieving takes on a completely different pattern.

It's important to release the disillusionment and anger when the glorified image of the mother is shattered. Simply ignoring the accompanying feelings and subconscious discomfort will not contribute to recovering your health. Instead of projecting your anger on someone else, or internalizing your anger, the more efficient way is to release the emotion through healthy habits like exercise, dietary management, breathing exercises, physical activity, crying, or venting with a safe friend.

Genuine forgiveness has a transformational effect on the forgiver. Forgiving in small doses allows the space for future forgiving when step by step the forgiver identifies and analyzes the issue to gain understanding. This will generate tranquility and awareness to identify dysfunctional behavior before it creates anxiety or frustration. In addition to this, the narcissistic mother will also be disarmed when she sees that her behavior does not have an intimidating effect anymore. The daughter will also be able to immediately spot red flags in the rest of her engaging community, friends, relationships, and workspaces.

So, what is the most efficient way to distance yourself from the narcissistic mother? How do you create separateness? The focus has to be on leaving the operational narcissistic system by limiting interaction and then cultivating healthy relationships where qualities like generosity, safety, reciprocity, sincerity, a sense of being wanted, empathy, discretion, and so forth, hold you supportively while you liberate yourself and embrace recovery. Getting involved in more nurturing connections where you are allowed to show up just as you are is a crucial step to healing. This process of harnessing the world back into your space of safety and trust definitely involves developing a working relationship with a therapist to guide you through the existing distortions. You can only reach a space of safety by sharing your own needs during continuous nonjudgmental exchanges where the risk of a loss of a relationship or an attack is diminished in contrast to the narcissistic system. The final step is to adapt your expectations once you know that the danger is over and that it is time to grieve.

Focus on the following steps to attain your liberation.

- Break the alliance and habit of going for help from the same person who breaks you.

- Make time for mindful and meaningful activities, and meditation.

- Don't let the grief confuse you. Don't ignore the grief. Grief is simply a natural process of letting go and it is only a little more complicated because you are grieving a complex narcissistic loss.

- Address your anxiety and depression with professional help. Improve contact with reliable significant others.

- Journaling your process, feelings, and thoughts is a helpful device to see your growth over time. It helps to maintain improvement and shows you how you have separated yourself from the trauma and grief.

- Acceptance brings resolution. Your rich life story makes you strong, don't deny it. Use it as a gift.

First, the physiological symptoms of post-traumatic stress disorder have been brought within manageable limits. Second, the person is able to bear the feelings associated with traumatic memories. Third, the person has authority over her memories; she can elect both to remember the trauma and to put memory aside. Fourth, the memory of the traumatic event is a coherent narrative, linked with feeling. Fifth, the person's damaged self-esteem has been restored. Sixth, the person's important relationships have been re-established. Seventh, and finally, the person has reconstructed a coherent system of meaning and belief that encompasses the story of trauma. – Judith Lewis Herman (Wright, 2018)

Takeaway Guidelines

- Forgiveness means reframing your concept of letting go.

- Your healing journey implies redefining your concept of the self, evaluating your circumstances, addressing overwhelming emotions to establish intelligence, releasing yourself from toxic shame by maintaining non-negotiable boundaries, soothing depression and anxiety, learning to speak up, and learning to ask for help.

- Grieving is a natural process. It is a useful process. It is a necessary process for making progress and finding tranquility.

Calls to Action

- Stop internalizing!

- You never had a mother. It's time to grieve the loss.

- Break the cycle.

- Attain your liberation.

- Use your newfound knowledge as a gift.

Conclusion

The past cannot be changed, only understood.
–Christine Hammond

The core concept of trauma is a reality. One that limits. One that defines. And one that repeats itself unless we deliberately silence it. The distorted imbalance of power with a primary caregiver who failed you needs to be restored. The conditioning of symptomatic reactions may start with a caregiver but it becomes a cumulative habit with other relationships in adult life that disrespect and damage your dignity as an individual human being.

To heal from this challenging interpersonal distress, you have to face your inner being and see the hurt from the unappreciated, undervalued little girl. You must find her, know her, understand her, and give her hope again through painfully intimate connection. You must commit to helping her, to embrace the poor choices combined with all her weaknesses of her shadow side. You must ultimately love her for who she is, for who she has become, despite the journey. This is the process of accepting the self.

"It is, after all, not necessary to fly right into the middle of the sun, but it is necessary to crawl to a clean little spot on earth where the sun sometimes shines and one can warm oneself a little" (Popova, 2015).

Taking Action to Break the Cycle

If you think it is unnecessary to take action, read Kafka's letter to his abusive narcissistic father dating back to 1919 and very much coined as the only and closest autobiography of the writer's life. (*Letter to his Father*, Franz Kafka) The book is a 47-page letter addressed to his father but in the end, his mother never delivered it to the abusive parent after Kafka entrusted her with the manuscript. His compulsive effort for a vain hope of understanding never reached his father's eyes. Perhaps his mother understood that his conciliatory attempts would ultimately fail and she spared him this additional disappointment… But ultimately, Kafka's literary legacy reveals to us the devastating effects of the toxic force of parental influence on a child's development. His life story makes it evident how the parental influence in the early stages of a child's life establishes the patterns and emotional habits that we exhibit in later relationships in our lives. It is up to you to break that cycle. It is up to you to prevent your offspring from suffering the same fate. It is up to you to open your eyes and see what the narcissistic parent can never see. You have a choice. We can choose to pretend that our past doesn't exist, but I have found that ignoring the pain only worsens the agony. We can choose to ignore our demons, or we can allow them to heal us. I prefer them to work for me, not the other way around.

Inspiration and Hope

Did the following words echo through your head while reading this book? Anger, sadness, grief, bitterness, victimization, entitlement, hypersensitivity, condescending, controlling, self-importance, manipulative, splitting, guilt-tripping, remorselessness, lying, deceitfulness, jealousy, competition, violations, emotional unavailability, cruelty, abusiveness, gaslighting. If so, it's time to make a change.

The narcissist's child sees the world in a fragmented form. Nothing is real. Nothing relates. Everything is made up of parts that float like gloomy images past the self that stands in utter isolation. It is time to make those fragmented memories a narrative, it is time to change the distorted reality. Facing and communicating our story makes us feel more integrated and whole. We gain insight into our responses and behaviors and recover a sense of calm to the narrative that was taken from us. We stop blaming ourselves, we eliminate painful experiences as we gradually process the trauma, until we are able to rewrite our stories in a more coherent way. We can never control the past but we can certainly manage the way we respond to it.

How do you see your future? Do you want this woman to become a battered version of the little girl or do you want to respect her for her resilience? Think about the legacy that you would like to leave behind for your siblings, children, your friends, your colleagues, your intimate partners. How do you want them to remember you when they stand at your grave? Think of one word that you would like to hear from them, and follow that course. Through your own healing, you inspire other people who hurt, you inspire future generations, you inspire survivors from the endless other forms of abuse. Through your healing, you give yourself and others a future.

Calls to Action

- You will defeat narcissism only if you understand

Conclusion

the narcissist's mind.

- Focus on your own protection against a toxic mother.

- Manage and maintain abusive relations.

- In the end, it is the relationship you have with yourself that saves you.

- Release.

- Relearn.

- Reinvent.

- Improve.

- Liberate.

- Breathe.

Thank You

Before you leave, I'd just like to say, thank you so much for purchasing my book.

I spent many days and nights working on this book so I could finally put this in your hands.

So, before you leave, I'd like to ask you a small favor.

Would you please consider posting a review on the platform? Your reviews are one of the best ways to support indie authors like me, and every review counts.

Your feedback will allow me to continue writing books just like this one, so let me know if you enjoyed it and why. I read every review and I would love to hear from you. Simply scan this QR code below to leave a review.

Scan the QR Code Below to Leave a Review:

References

A Knight's Tale (2001) - IMDb. (n.d.). IMDB. https://www.imdb.com/title/tt0183790/quotes/qt1694763

Ackerman, C. E. (2018, July 12). *What is Self-Acceptance? 25 Exercises + Definition and Quotes.* PositivePsychology.com. https://positivepsychology.com/self-acceptance/

Atkinson, A. (2020). *63 Most Common Things Narcissistic Mothers Say.* MindJournal. https://themindsjournal.com/things-narcissistic-mothers-say/

Brian, P. (2022, January 17). *10 signs of the golden child syndrome (+ what to do about it).* Ideapod. https://ideapod.com/golden-child-syndrome/

Brickel, R. E. (2021, September 21). *Injured, Not Broken: Why It's So Hard to Know You Have CPTSD.* PsychAlive.

Brickel, R. E., MA, & LMFT. (2019, June 4). *Why a Bottom-Up Approach to Trauma Therapy is So Powerful.* Brickel and Associates LLC. https://brickelandassociates.com/bottom-up-approach-to-trauma/

Casale, S., & Banchi, V. (2020). Narcissism and problematic social media use: A systematic literature review. *Addictive Behaviors Reports*, *11*, 100252. https://doi.org/10.1016/j.abrep.2020.100252

Chadwick, B. (2022, May 9). *Narcissist Apocalypse: How to Differentiate the Overlapping Behaviors of ADHD & Narcissist Abuse - Q&A With Dr. Amelia Kelley on Apple Podcasts*. Apple Podcasts. https://podcasts.apple.com/za/podcast/narcissist-apocalypse/id1452117002?i=1000548548744

Cherry, K. (2019, July 17). *Uninvolved Parenting and Its Effects on Children*. Verywell Mind. https://www.verywellmind.com/what-is-uninvolved-parenting-2794958

Community, I. L. (n.d.). *IBCCES Learning Community*. IBCCES Learning Community. https://ibcces.org/learning/what-are-the-effects-of-emotional-abuse/

Curtis, C. (2018, August 3). *I Know Why the Caged Bird Sings Quotes with Page Number | FreebookSummary*. Study Guides and Book Summaries. https://freebooksummary.com/i-know-why-the-caged-bird-sings-quotes-with-page-number-118105

Dewar, G. (2017, July 2). *The authoritative parenting style: An evidence-based guide*. PARENTING SCIENCE. https://parentingscience.com/authoritative-parenting-style/

DSM-IV and DSM-5 Criteria for the Personality Disorders. (2012). https://www.nyu.edu/gsas/dept/philo/courses/materials/Narc.Pers.DSM.pdf

engulfing mother - daughters of narcissistic mothers. (2022, January 13). Understanding and Healing for Daughters of Narcissistic Mothers. https://www.daughtersofnarcissisticmothers.com/engulfing-mother/

References

Firestone, L. (2018, August 7). *PsychAlive*. PsychAlive. https://www.psychalive.org/

Fox, D. D. (2020, November 7). *Children of Narcissistic Parents*. YouTube. https://www.youtube.com/watch?v=Vjz6rTG3wao

Gaslighting - daughters of narcissistic mothers. (n.d.). Understanding and Healing for Daughters of Narcissistic Mothers. https://www.daughtersofnarcissisticmothers.com/gaslighting/

Gaslighting Examples: The Most Covert Abuse Used by a Narcissistic Mother. (2021, August 4). Raging Female. https://ragingfemale.com/gaslighting-examples-narcissistic-mother/

Grande, D. T. (2018a, May 10). *What is the Difference Between PTSD and Complex PTSD (C-PTSD)?* YouTube. https://www.youtube.com/watch?v=T41Pn3rIis4

Grande, D. T. (2018b, May 29). *What Causes Narcissistic Personality Disorder? - YouTube*. YouTube. https://www.youtube.com/watch?v=5cK4z4cYQLY

Grande, D. T. (2019a). Grandiose & Vulnerable Narcissism: Which is worse? Is Recovery Possible? [YouTube Video]. YouTube. https://www.youtube.com/watch?v=E0e5kKdXl10

Grande, D. T. (2019b, July 11). *Nine Signs of the Narcissistic Mother | Mother-Daughter Relationships*. YouTube. https://youtu.be/0eG4oldh2x8

Grande, D. T. (2019c, September 13). *Forgiving the Narcissist | Empathy, Rejection, and Negativity*. YouTube. https://youtu.be/msAu6N-xuGM

Grande, D. T. (2019d, September 29). *Grandiose Narcissism and Shame.* YouTube. https://www.youtube.com/watch?v=yNqpPU1_WYk

Grande, D. T. (2019e, October 13). *How Can a Narcissist Change? | Is Lack of Insight Invariable?* YouTube. https://www.youtube.com/watch?v=yslqpRTI4iU

Grande, Dr. T. (2018). What is the Difference Between Borderline Personality Disorder and Complex PTSD (C-PTSD)? YouTube. https://www.youtube.com/watch?v=aUv-_3aiNTc

Grande, Dr. T. (2019a). Is Complex PTSD different than Comorbid BPD & PTSD? YouTube. https://www.youtube.com/watch?v=tECAgLPLrZY

Grande, Dr. T. (2019b, August 20). *10 Signs of a daughter with High Trait Narcissism.* YouTube. https://www.youtube.com/watch?v=Hy3j6ZJidV8

Grande, Dr. T. (2020, May 7). *3 Types of a daughter / Narcissistic Mother Relationship.* YouTube. https://www.youtube.com/watch?v=lPAZTF2mja8&t=140s

Hammond, C. (2016, July 21). *7 Steps in Healing from a Narcissistic Parent.* Psych Central. https://psychcentral.com/pro/exhausted-woman/2016/07/7-steps-in-healing-from-a-narcissistic-parent#1

Hammond, C. (2020, January 21). *7 Ways a Narcissistic Attachment Is Destructive.* Psych Central. https://psychcentral.com/pro/exhausted-woman/2020/01/7-ways-a-narcissistic-attachment-is-destructive#3

Hampton, D. (2014, September 10). *Neuroplasticity: Are You Making a Masterpiece or Mess of Your Brain?* The Best Brain

Possible. https://thebestbrainpossible.com/masterpiece-or-mess/

Hartney, E. (2008, November 14). *The Cycle of Sexual Abuse and Abusive Adult Relationships.* Verywell Mind. https://www.verywellmind.com/the-cycle-of-sexual-abuse-22460

How to heal from excess feminine energy after narc abuse. (2018, March 15). YouTube. https://www.youtube.com/watch?v=70Y9vc8m1E8

Introduction to Personality Disorders. (2022). Mental Help. https://www.mentalhelp.net/personality-disorders/

Irina. (2019, September 9). *How Grieving the Loss of the Dream can Heal You.* Love Grow Be Happy. https://www.lovegrowbehappy.com/how-the-loss-of-the-dream-can-heal/

Jabeen, F., Gerritsen, C., & Treur, J. (2021). Healing the next generation: an adaptive agent model for the effects of parental narcissism. *Brain Informatics*, *8*(1). https://doi.org/10.1186/s40708-020-00115-z

Jack, C. (2021, January 12). *Sons and Daughters of Narcissistic Mothers: Who Fares Worse?* Psychology Today. https://www.psychologytoday.com/intl/blog/women-autism-spectrum-disorder/202101/sons-and-daughters-narcissistic-mothers-who-fares-worse

Lancer, D. (2019). *How to Confront Narcissists' Lethal Weapon: Projection.* Psychology Today. https://www.psychologytoday.com/us/blog/toxic-relationships/201903/how-confront-narcissists-lethal-weapon-projection

Launder, A. (2020, February 13). *The Impact of Growing Up with a Narcissistic Parent*. The Awareness Centre. https://theawarenesscentre.com/narcissistic-parent/

Maercker, A. (2021). Development of the new CPTSD diagnosis for ICD-11. *Borderline Personality Disorder and Emotion Dysregulation*, *8*(1). BMC. https://doi.org/10.1186/s40479-021-00148-8

Mandal, Dr. A. (2010, July 12). *Heritability of Narcissism*. News-Medical. https://www.news-medical.net/health/Heritability-of-Narcissism.aspx

Martinez-Lewi, L. (2019). *The Narcissist in Your Life Podcast: Healing and Restoration from Childhood Re-Traumatization by High Level Narcissists on Apple Podcasts*. Apple Podcasts. https://podcasts.apple.com/za/podcast/the-narcissist-in-your-life-podcast/id1278783469?i=1000556674475

Mayer, B. A. (2021, July 27). *Do You Have a Dark Side? Shadow Work Experts Say Yes*. Healthline. https://www.healthline.com/health/mental-health/shadow-work#benefits

Mayo Clinic. (2017). *Fibromyalgia - symptoms and causes*. Mayo Clinic. https://www.mayoclinic.org/diseases-conditions/fibromyalgia/symptoms-causes/syc-20354780

Mayo Clinic Staff. (2018, July 6). *Post-traumatic stress disorder (PTSD) - Symptoms and Causes*. Mayo Clinic. https://www.mayoclinic.org/diseases-conditions/post-traumatic-stress-disorder/symptoms-causes/syc-20355967

MedCircle. (2019). BPD vs. CPTSD: How to Spot the Differences. YouTube. https://www.youtube.com/watch?v=87UhgkE4-qU

Mindmadeeasy. (2021, March 8). *What is the Polyvagal Theory?* YouTube. https://www.youtube.com/watch?v=zYvZUorQbrg

Moore, A. (2020, November 16). *"You're Too Sensitive" & Other Common Phrases Used by Gaslighting Parents.* Mindbodygreen. https://www.mindbodygreen.com/articles/signs-of-gaslighting-parents/

Moore, C. (2019, May 26). *The Positive Psychology of Gratitude and Trauma - Narcissist Abuse Support.* Narcissist Abuse Support. https://narcissistabusesupport.com/the-positive-psychology-of-gratitude-and-trauma/

Nafeesah, A. (2022, March 13). *This Dark Personality Type Is a Master Manipulator: 6 Signs You've Met One.* Mindbodygreen. https://www.mindbodygreen.com/articles/machiavellianism

Neo, P. (2020, July 16). *How A Relationship with a Narcissist Can Cause Lifelong Trauma + How to Heal.* Mindbodygreen. https://www.mindbodygreen.com/articles/how-narcissist-relationships-can-cause-trauma/

Ni, P. (2016). *10 Signs of a Narcissistic Parent.* Psychology Today. https://www.psychologytoday.com/us/blog/communication-success/201602/10-signs-narcissistic-parent

Patricia. (2021a, March 25). *How To Set Boundaries with a Narcissist.* Inner Toxic Relief. https://innertoxicrelief.com/how-to-set-boundaries-with-a-narcissist/

Patricia. (2021b, April 15). *5 Ways to Respond to Narcissistic Rage.* Inner Toxic Relief. https://innertoxicrelief.com/respond-to-narcissistic-rage/

Patricia. (2022, February 17). *19 Steps to Prepare for Low-Contact with a Narcissistic Mother.* Inner Toxic Relief.

https://innertoxicrelief.com/prepare-for-low-contact-with-a-narcissistic-mother/

Paulhus, D. L., & Williams, K. M. (2002). The Dark Triad of personality: Narcissism, Machiavellianism, and psychopathy. *Journal of Research in Personality*, *36*(6), 556–563. ScienceDirect. https://doi.org/10.1016/s0092-6566(02)00505-6

Plath, S. (2005). *The Bell Jar*. Faber And Faber. (Original work published 1963)

Popova, M. (2012, March 2). *What Is Character? Debunking the Myth of Fixed Personality*. The Marginalian. https://www.themarginalian.org/2012/03/02/character-personality/

Popova, M. (2015, March 5). *Kafka's Remarkable Letter to His Abusive and Narcissistic Father*. The Marginalian. https://www.themarginalian.org/2015/03/05/franz-kafka-letter-father/

Porges, D. S. (2018). Dr. Stephen Porges: What is the Polyvagal Theory [YouTube Video]. YouTube. https://www.youtube.com/watch?v=ec3AUMDjtKQ

Quintana, S. (2021, January 29). *What Narcissistic Abuse Does to a Woman*. The Virago. https://medium.com/the-virago/what-narcissistic-abuse-does-to-a-woman-3b4e3f16b780

Quirke, M. G. (2019, August 5). *Complex PTSD and Dissociation: How the Mind Copes with Trauma*. Michael G. Quirke, MFT. https://michaelgquirke.com/complex-ptsd-and-dissociation-how-the-mind-copes-with-trauma/

Quirke, M. G. (2020a, October 6). *Complex PTSD and Chronic Pain: Exploring the Connection*. Michael G. Quirke, MFT. https://michaelgquirke.com/complex-ptsd-and-chronic-pain-exploring-the-connection/

References

Quirke, M. G. (2020b, October 14). *Recovering from Complex PTSD: 3 Key Stages of Long-Term Healing*. Michael G. Quirke, MFT. https://michaelgquirke.com/recovering-from-complex-ptsd-3-key-stages-of-long-term-healing/

Quirke, M. G. (2021a, May 9). *Signs You Had a Narcissistic Parent & What Trauma Treatment Can Do to Help*. Michael G. Quirke, MFT. https://michaelgquirke.com/signs-you-had-a-narcissistic-parent-what-trauma-treatment-can-do-to-help/

Quirke, M. G. (2021b, June 14). *Your Narcissistic Parent, CPTSD, & Toxic Shame*. Michael G. Quirke, MFT. https://michaelgquirke.com/the-relationship-between-your-narcissistic-parent-cptsd-toxic-shame/

Ramani, D. (2019, October 4). *Narcissistic family roles (scapegoat, golden child, invisible child)*. YouTube. https://www.youtube.com/watch?v=Rn3xhDni4w4&t=379s

Ramani, D. (2020a, April 12). *What is "triangulation"? (Glossary of Narcissistic Relationships)*. YouTube. https://youtu.be/qS4knTxthuI

Ramani, D. (2020b, May 10). *Narcissistic Mothers*. YouTube. https://www.youtube.com/watch?v=VedPxLtgcLE

Ramani, D. (2020c, June 16). *Narcissists and the Silent Treatment*. YouTube. https://youtu.be/o8Cv5tSE6RI

Ramani, D. (2020d, August 12). *How to deal with grief from narcissistic relationships*. YouTube. https://youtu.be/K21JcsaEhW0

Ramani, D. (2020e, August 26). *Dealing with the overwhelming fatigue of a narcissistic relationship*. YouTube. https://youtu.be/Ert2O2sozhw

Ramani, D. (2021a, June 30). *What happens to the scapegoat in adulthood?* YouTube. https://www.youtube.com/watch?v=GjWR5WlYWVM

Ramani, D. (2021b, July 12). *When the invisible child grows up...* YouTube. https://www.youtube.com/watch?v=aIfg3G_iA-Q

Ramani, D. (2021c, August 3). *When the golden child grows up.* YouTube. https://youtu.be/tdn30HxQB_w

Reid, J. (2019, August 7). *The narcissistic family's scapegoat: Survival and Recovery.* Jay Reid Psychotherapy. https://jreidtherapy.com/scapegoated-by-narcissistic-parent/

Reid, J. (2021, July 21). *The power of grief after leaving the narcissistic family.* YouTube. https://youtu.be/1XGxk3HzqIA

Reid, J. (2022, April 17). *Giving up the quest to prove the narcissist wrong about you.* YouTube. https://youtu.be/LQlUoMud0Do

Rhodewalt, F. (2019). narcissism | Definition, Origins, Pathology, & Behavior. In *Encyclopædia Britannica.* https://www.britannica.com/science/narcissism

Robins, A. (2020, April 27). *Trauma Bonds: How a Narcissistic Mother Primes You for Abuse.* Invisible Illness. https://medium.com/invisible-illness/trauma-bonds-how-a-narcissistic-mother-primes-you-for-abuse-8987b4984361

Russ, E., Shedler, J., Bradley, R., & Westen, D. (2008). Refining the Construct of Narcissistic Personality Disorder: Diagnostic Criteria and Subtypes. *American Journal of Psychiatry, 165*(11), 1473–1481. https://doi.org/10.1176/appi.ajp.2008.07030376

Salters-Pedneault, K. (2020, August 28). *Understanding Cluster B Personality Disorders in the DSM-5.* Verywell Mind. https://www.verywellmind.com/the-cluster-b-personality-disorders-425429

References

Schwartz, A. (n.d.). *On the Family as a System and the Problem of Triangulation - Family Issues and Relationship Issues Topic Center.* MentalHelp. https://www.mentalhelp.net/blogs/on-the-family-as-a-system-and-the-problem-of-triangulation/

Schwartz, A. (2015). *The Narcissist Versus the narcissistic personality disorder - Personality Disorders.* Mentalhelp. https://www.mentalhelp.net/blogs/the-narcissist-versus-the-narcissistic-personality-disorder/

Steber, C. (2019, August 7). *Is My Mother Gaslighting Me? 9 Signs of This Manipulation Tactic, According to Experts.* Bustle. https://www.bustle.com/p/is-my-mother-gaslighting-me-9-signs-of-this-manipulation-tactic-according-to-experts-18551081

Stines, Dr. S. (2018, June 4). *When you grow up as the invisible child (the impact of being raised by a narcissist).* Psych Central. https://psychcentral.com/pro/recovery-expert/2018/06/when-you-grow-up-as-the-invisible-child#How-do-you-heal-from-being-invisible?

Streep, P. (2015). *8 Toxic Patterns in Mother-Daughter Relationships.* Psychology Today. https://www.psychologytoday.com/us/blog/tech-support/201502/8-toxic-patterns-in-mother-daughter-relationships

Tedx Talks. (2019, May 3). *Finding Happiness: How Forgiving my Mother Radically Changed My Life | Sonia Weyers | TEDxFHNW.* YouTube. https://youtu.be/3I4R_em_6wE

The School of Life. (2020). 12 signs you might be suffering from PTSD. YouTube. https://www.youtube.com/watch?v=qOibW5LXt3w

Valentini, K. (2019, May 31). *Jung's Shadow and Narcissists | Psychology Today.* Www.psychologytoday.com.

https://www.psychologytoday.com/intl/blog/destructive-relationships/201905/jung-s-shadow-and-narcissists

van Schie, C. C., Jarman, H. L., Huxley, E., & Grenyer, B. F. S. (2020). Narcissistic traits in young people: understanding the role of parenting and maltreatment. *Borderline Personality Disorder and Emotion Dysregulation*, *7*(1). https://doi.org/10.1186/s40479-020-00125-7

What Happens to the Golden Child When the Narcissistic Mother Dies? | OptimistMinds. (2020, December 8). OptimistMinds. https://optimistminds.com/what-happens-to-the-golden-child-when-the-narcissistic-mother-dies/

Wright, A. (2018, July 8). *All The Little Fragments: Understanding Complex Relational Trauma*. Annie Wright, LMFT. https://www.anniewright.com/all-the-little-fragments-understanding-complex-relational-trauma/

Yearwood, K. M. (2019, November 22). *3 Benefits of Shadow Work During Recovery After Narcissistic Abuse*. Karin Yearwood's BrokenFlowerPots. https://medium.com/brokenflowerpots/3-benefits-of-shadow-work-during-recovery-after-narcissistic-abuse-cc34943e6635

Printed in Great Britain
by Amazon